JavaScript Unlocked

Improve your code's maintainability, performance, and security through practical expert insights and unlock the full potential of JavaScript

Dmitry Sheiko

PUBLISHING

BIRMINGHAM - MUMBAI

JavaScript Unlocked

First published: December 2015

Production reference: 1011215

Published by Packt Publishing Ltd.
Livery Place
35 Livery Street
Birmingham B3 2PB, UK.

ISBN 978-1-78588-157-2

www.packtpub.com

Credits

Author
Dmitry Sheiko

Reviewer
Durgesh Priyaranjan

Commissioning Editor
Wilson Dsouza

Acquisition Editor
Meeta Rajani

Content Development Editor
Priyanka Mehta

Technical Editor
Mohita Vyas

Copy Editor
Kausambhi Majumdar

Project Coordinator
Izzat Contractor

Proofreader
Safis Editing

Indexer
Tejal Soni

Graphics
Abhinash Sahu

Production Coordinator
Aparna Bhagat

Cover Work
Aparna Bhagat

About the Author

Dmitry Sheiko is a passionate blogger and the author of *Instant Testing with QUnit*.

Dmitry got hooked to computer programming in the late '80s. For the last 18 years, he has been in web development. His very first open source contribution was an XSLT-based CMS in 2004. Since then, he has been contributing quite a lot to FOSS. You can find Dmitry's latest works at `https://github.com/dsheiko`. Currently, he is working as a web developer in the lovely city of Frankfurt am Main at Crytek GmbH.

First, I would like to thank my family for the continuous support and letting me to realize my potential. A special thank you to my father, who took me to an industrial computer center when I was 3 years old. In I decade after this, with the advance in PCs, I realized that computers mean games, and after a while, I became curious enough to understand how the games are built. This is how I started learning programming.

Thank you to my team at Crytek, who compliantly follow all the practices described in the book and adapt to the constantly evolving technologies to keep up with the pace I set.

About the Reviewer

Durgesh Priyaranjan is a senior software developer who has been working on various technologies. However, he loves JavaScript programming and interaction design the most. He is currently based in Bengaluru (India) and is working as a UI engineer for one of the Indian e-commerce giants, Flipkart.

He loves trying out different technologies without any bias. Of late, he can be found tinkering around with Raspberry Pi.

I'd like to thank my loving wife for her continuous support of my work and work-related hobbies.

www.PacktPub.com

Support files, eBooks, discount offers, and more

For support files and downloads related to your book, please visit www.PacktPub.com.

Did you know that Packt offers eBook versions of every book published, with PDF and ePub files available? You can upgrade to the eBook version at www.PacktPub.com and as a print book customer, you are entitled to a discount on the eBook copy. Get in touch with us at service@packtpub.com for more details.

At www.PacktPub.com, you can also read a collection of free technical articles, sign up for a range of free newsletters and receive exclusive discounts and offers on Packt books and eBooks.

https://www2.packtpub.com/books/subscription/packtlib

Do you need instant solutions to your IT questions? PacktLib is Packt's online digital book library. Here, you can search, access, and read Packt's entire library of books.

Why subscribe?

- Fully searchable across every book published by Packt
- Copy and paste, print, and bookmark content
- On demand and accessible via a web browser

Free access for Packt account holders

If you have an account with Packt at www.PacktPub.com, you can use this to access PacktLib today and view 9 entirely free books. Simply use your login credentials for immediate access.

Table of Contents

Preface

JavaScript was born as a scripting language at the most inappropriate time—the time of browser wars. It was neglected and misunderstood for a decade and endured six editions. And look at it now! JavaScript has become a mainstream programming language. It has advanced literally everywhere: in large-scale client-side development, server scripting, desktop applications, native mobile programming, game development, DB querying, hardware control, and OS automating. JavaScript acquired a number of subsets such as Objective-J, CoffeeScript, TypeScript, and others. JavaScript is marvelously concise and an expressive language. It features prototype-based OOP, object composition and inheritance, variadic functions, event-driven programming, and non-blocking I/O. However, to exploit the true power of JavaScript, we need to have a deep understanding of language quirks. Moreover, while developing in JavaScript, we will become aware of its numerous pitfalls, and we will need a few tricks to avoid them. The project formerly known as EcmaScript Harmony, was just recently finalized in the specification named EcmaScript 2015, which is more often referred to as ES6. This not only brought the language to the next level, but also introduced a number of new technologies that require attention.

This book aims to guide the reader in understanding the upcoming and existing features of JavaScript. It is fully packed with code recipes that address common programming tasks. The tasks are supplied with solutions for classical JavaScript (ES5) as well as for the next generation language (ES6-7). The book doesn't focus only on in-browser language, but also provides the essentials on writing efficient JavaScript for desktop applications, server-side software, and native module apps. The ultimate goal of the author is not just to describe the language, but also to help the reader to improve their code for better maintainability, readability, and performance.

What this book covers

Chapter 1, Diving into the JavaScript Core, discusses the techniques to improve the expressiveness of the code, to master multi-line strings and templating, and to manipulate arrays and array-like objects. The chapter explains how to take advantage of JavaScript prototype without harming the readability your code. Further, the chapter introduces the "magic methods" of JavaScript and gives a practical example of their use.

Chapter 2, Modular Programming with JavaScript, describes the modularity in JavaScript: what modules are, why they are important, the standard approaches for asynchronously and synchronously loaded modules, and what ES6 modules are. The chapter shows how CommonJS modules are used in server-side JavaScript and how to pre-compile them for in-browser use. It elaborates how asynchronous and synchronous approaches can be combined to achieve a better application performance. It also explains how one can polyfill ES6 modules for production by the means of Babel.js.

Chapter 3, DOM Scripting and AJAX, introduces Document Object Model (DOM), shows the best practices to minimize browser reflow, and enhance application performance while operating with the DOM. The chapter also compares two client-server communication models: XHR and Fetch API.

Chapter 4, HTML5 APIs, considers the persistence APIs of the browser such as Web Storage, IndexDB, and FileSystem. It introduces Web Components and gives a walk-through of the creation of a custom component. The chapter describes server-to-browser communication APIs such as SSE and WebSockets.

Chapter 5, Asynchronous JavaScript, explains the nonblocking nature of JavaScript, elaborates the event loop and the call stack. The chapter considers the popular styles of chaining asynchronous calls and handling errors. It presents the async/ await technique of ES7 and also gives examples of running tasks in parallel and in sequence using the Promise API and the Async.js library. It describes throttling and debouncing concepts.

Chapter 6, A Large-Scale JavaScript Application Architecture, focuses on code maintainability and architecture. The chapter introduces the MVC paradigm and its derivatives, MVP and MVVM. It also shows, with examples, how concern separation is implemented in popular frameworks such as Backbone.js, AngularJS, and ReactJS.

Chapter 7, JavaScript Beyond the Browser, explains how to write command-line programs in JavaScript and how to build a web server with Node.js. It also covers the creation of desktop HTML5 applications with NW.js and guides the development of native mobile applications with Phongap.

Chapter 8, Debugging and Profiling, dives into bug detection and isolation. It examines the capacities of DevTools and the lesser-known features of the JavaScript console API.

What you need for this book

It's enough if you have a modern browser and a text editor to run the examples from the book. It maybe helpful, however, to use a browser tool similar to Firefox Scratchpad (`https://developer.mozilla.org/en-US/docs/Tools/Scratchpad`) to edit the sample code directly in the browser. The books also contains ES6/ES7 code examples that rely on features not yet available in browsers. You can run these examples in Babel.js's online sandbox available at `https://babeljs.io/repl/`.

You will find detailed instructions of how to set up your development environment and install the required tools and dependencies in the chapters where we refer to Node.js, NW.js, PhoneGap, JavaScript frameworks, and NPM packages.

Who this book is for

This book is for the developers who are already familiar with JavaScript and want to level up their skills to get the most out of the language. The book is practice-oriented and would be helpful for those who are used to the "learn by doing" approach, as the topics are thoroughly covered with real-life examples and tutorials.

Conventions

In this book, you will find a number of text styles that distinguish between different kinds of information. Here are some examples of these styles and an explanation of their meaning.

Code words in text, database table names, folder names, filenames, file extensions, pathnames, dummy URLs, user input, and Twitter handles are shown as follows: "We can include other contexts through the use of the `include` directive."

A block of code is set as follows:

```
var res = [ 1, 2, 3, 4 ].filter(function( v ){
 return v > 2;
})
console.log( res ); // [3,4]
```

When we wish to draw your attention to a particular part of a code block, the relevant lines or items are set in bold:

```
/**
 * @param {Function} [cb] - callback
 */
function fn( cb ) {
 cb && cb();
};
```

Any command-line input or output is written as follows:

```
npm install fs-walk cli-color
```

New terms and **important words** are shown in bold. Words that you see on the screen, for example, in menus or dialog boxes, appear in the text like this: "As soon as *Enter* is pressed, the console outputs **I'm running**."

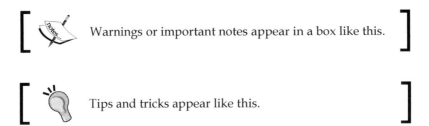

Warnings or important notes appear in a box like this.

Tips and tricks appear like this.

Reader feedback

Feedback from our readers is always welcome. Let us know what you think about this book—what you liked or disliked. Reader feedback is important for us as it helps us develop titles that you will really get the most out of.

To send us general feedback, simply e-mail feedback@packtpub.com, and mention the book's title in the subject of your message.

If there is a topic that you have expertise in and you are interested in either writing or contributing to a book, see our author guide at www.packtpub.com/authors.

Customer support

Now that you are the proud owner of a Packt book, we have a number of things to help you to get the most from your purchase.

Downloading the example code

You can download the example code files from your account at http://www. packtpub.com for all the Packt Publishing books you have purchased. If you purchased this book elsewhere, you can visit http://www.packtpub.com/support and register to have the files e-mailed directly to you.

Errata

Although we have taken every care to ensure the accuracy of our content, mistakes do happen. If you find a mistake in one of our books — maybe a mistake in the text or the code — we would be grateful if you could report this to us. By doing so, you can save other readers from frustration and help us improve subsequent versions of this book. If you find any errata, please report them by visiting http://www.packtpub. com/submit-errata, selecting your book, clicking on the **Errata Submission Form** link, and entering the details of your errata. Once your errata are verified, your submission will be accepted and the errata will be uploaded to our website or added to any list of existing errata under the Errata section of that title.

To view the previously submitted errata, go to https://www.packtpub.com/books/ content/support and enter the name of the book in the search field. The required information will appear under the **Errata** section.

Piracy

Piracy of copyrighted material on the Internet is an ongoing problem across all media. At Packt, we take the protection of our copyright and licenses very seriously. If you come across any illegal copies of our works in any form on the Internet, please provide us with the location address or website name immediately so that we can pursue a remedy.

Please contact us at copyright@packtpub.com with a link to the suspected pirated material.

We appreciate your help in protecting our authors and our ability to bring you valuable content.

Questions

If you have a problem with any aspect of this book, you can contact us at
questions@packtpub.com, and we will do our best to address the problem.

1
Diving into the JavaScript Core

You may have owned an iPhone for years and regard yourself as an experienced user. At the same time, you keep removing unwanted characters one at a time while typing by pressing delete. However, one day you find out that a quick shake allows you to delete the whole message in one tap. Then you wonder why on earth you didn't know this earlier. The same thing happens with programming. We can be quite satisfied with our coding until, all of sudden, we run into a trick or a lesser-known language feature that makes us reconsider the entire work done over the years. It turns out that we could do this in a cleaner, more readable, more testable, and more maintainable way. So it's presumed that you already have experience with JavaScript; however, this chapter equips you with the best practices to improve your code. We will cover the following topics:

- Making your code readable and expressive
- Mastering multiline strings in JavaScript
- Manipulating arrays in the ES5 way
- Traversing an object in an elegant, reliable, safe, and fast way
- The most effective way of declaring objects
- How to magic methods in JavaScript

Make your code readable and expressive

There are numerous practices and heuristics to make a code more readable, expressive, and clean. We will cover this topic later on, but here we will talk about syntactic sugar. The term means an alternative syntax that makes the code more expressive and readable. In fact, we already had some of this in JavaScript from the very beginning. For instance, the increment/decrement and addition/subtraction assignment operators inherited from C. *foo++* is syntactic sugar for *foo = foo + 1*, and *foo += bar* is a shorter form for *foo = foo + bar*. Besides, we have a few tricks that serve the same purpose.

JavaScript applies logical expressions to so-called **short-circuit** evaluation. This means that an expression is read left to right, but as soon as the condition result is determined at an early stage, the expression tail is not evaluated. If we have *true || false || false*, the interpreter will know from the first test that the result is true regardless of other tests. So the *false || false* part is not evaluated, and this opens a way for creativity.

Function argument default value

When we need to specify default values for parameters we can do like that:

```
function stub( foo ) {
 return foo || "Default value";
}

console.log( stub( "My value" ) ); // My value
console.log( stub() ); // Default value
```

What is going on here? When `foo` is `true` (not `undefined`, NaN, `null`, `false`, 0, or `""`), the result of the logical expression is `foo` otherwise the expression is evaluated until `Default value` and this is the final result.

Starting with 6th edition of EcmaScript (specification of JavaScript language) we can use nicer syntax:

```
function stub( foo = "Default value" ) {
 return foo;
}
```

Conditional invocation

While composing our code we shorten it on conditions:"

```
var age = 20;
age >= 18 && console.log( "You are allowed to play this game" );
age >= 18 || console.log( "The game is restricted to 18 and over" );
```

In the preceding example, we used the AND (`&&`) operator to invoke `console.log` if the left-hand condition is Truthy. The OR (`||`) operator does the opposite, it calls `console.log` if the condition is `Falsy`.

I think the most common case in practice is the shorthand condition where the function is called only when it is provided:

```
/**
 * @param {Function} [cb] - callback
 */
function fn( cb ) {
 cb && cb();
};
```

The following is one more example on this:

```
/**
 * @class AbstractFoo
 */
AbstractFoo = function(){
 // call this.init if the subclass has init method
 this.init && this.init();
};
```

Syntactic sugar was introduced to its full extent to the JavaScript world only with the advance in CoffeeScript, a subset of the language that trans-compiles (compiles source-to-source) into JavaScript. Actually CoffeeScript, inspired by Ruby, Python, and Haskell, has unlocked arrow-functions, spreads, and other syntax to JavaScript developers. In 2011, Brendan Eich (the author of JavaScript) admitted that CoffeeScript influenced him in his work on EcmaScript Harmony, which was finalized this summer in ECMA-262 6th edition specification. From a marketing perspective, the specification writers agreed on using a new name convention that calls the 6th edition as EcmaScript 2015 and the 7th edition as EcmaScript 2016. Yet the community is used to abbreviations such as ES6 and ES7. To avoid confusion further in the book, we will refer to the specifications by these names. Now we can look at how this affects the new JavaScript.

Arrow functions

Traditional function expression may look like this:

```
function( param1, param2 ){ /* function body */ }
```

When declaring an expression using the arrow function (aka fat arrow function) syntax, we will have this in a less verbose form, as shown in the following:

```
( param1, param2 ) => { /* function body */ }
```

In my opinion, we don't gain much with this. But if we need, let's say, an array method callback, the traditional form would be as follows:

```
function( param1, param2 ){ return expression; }
```

Now the equivalent arrow function becomes shorter, as shown here:

```
( param1, param2 ) => expression
```

We may do filtering in an array this way:

```
// filter all the array elements greater than 2
var res = [ 1, 2, 3, 4 ].filter(function( v ){
 return v > 2;
})
console.log( res ); // [3,4]
```

Using an array function, we can do filtering in a cleaner form:

```
var res  = [ 1, 2, 3, 4 ].filter( v => v > 2 );
console.log( res ); // [3,4]
```

Besides shorter function declaration syntax, the arrow functions bring the so called lexical `this`. Instead of creating its own context, it uses the context of the surrounding object as shown here:

```
"use strict";
/**
* @class View
*/
let View = function(){
 let button = document.querySelector( "[data-bind=\"btn\"]" );
 /**
  * Handle button clicked event
  * @private
  */
```

```
  this.onClick = function(){
    console.log( "Button clicked" );
  };
  button.addEventListener( "click", () => {
    // we can safely refer surrounding object members
    this.onClick();
  }, false );
}
```

In the preceding example, we subscribed a handler function to a DOM event (`click`). Within the scope of the handler, we still have access to the view context (`this`), so we don't need to bind the handler to the outer scope or pass it as a variable through the closure:

```
var that = this;
button.addEventListener( "click", function(){
  // cross-cutting concerns
  that.onClick();
}, false );
```

Method definitions

As mentioned in the preceding section, arrow functions can be quite handy when declaring small inline callbacks, but always applying it for a shorter syntax is controversial. However, ES6 provides new alternative method definition syntax besides the arrow functions. The old-school method declaration may look as follows:

```
var foo = {
 bar: function( param1, param2 ) {
 }
}
```

In ES6 we can get rid of the function keyword and the colon. So the preceding code can be put this way:

```
let foo = {
 bar ( param1, param2 ) {
 }
}
```

The rest operator

Another syntax structure that was borrowed from CoffeeScript came to JavaScript as the rest operator (albeit, the approach is called *splats* in CoffeeScript).

When we had a few mandatory function parameters and an unknown number of rest parameters, we used to do something like this:

```
"use strict";
var cb = function() {
 // all available parameters into an array
 var args = [].slice.call( arguments ),
     // the first array element to foo and shift
     foo = args.shift(),
     // the new first array element to bar and shift
     bar = args.shift();
 console.log( foo, bar, args );
};
cb( "foo", "bar", 1, 2, 3 ); // foo bar [1, 2, 3]
```

Now check out how expressive this code becomes in ES6:

```
let cb = function( foo, bar, ...args ) {
 console.log( foo, bar, args );
}
cb( "foo", "bar", 1, 2, 3 ); // foo bar [1, 2, 3]
```

Function parameters aren't the only application of the rest operator. For example, we can use it in destructions as well, as follows:

```
let [ bar, ...others ] = [ "bar", "foo", "baz", "qux" ];
console.log([ bar, others ]); // ["bar",["foo","baz","qux"]]
```

The spread operator

Similarly, we can spread array elements into arguments:

```
let args = [ 2015, 6, 17 ],
    relDate = new Date( ...args );
console.log( relDate.toString() );  // Fri Jul 17 2015 00:00:00
GMT+0200 (CEST)
```

ES6 also provides expressive syntactic sugar for object creation and inheritance, but we will examine this later in *The most effective way of declaring objects* section.

Mastering multiline strings in JavaScript

Multi-line strings aren't a good part of JavaScript. While they are easy to declare in other languages (for instance, NOWDOC), you cannot just keep single-quoted or double-quoted strings in multiple lines. This will lead to syntax error as every line in JavaScript is considered as a possible command. You can set backslashes to show your intention:

```
var str = "Lorem ipsum dolor sit amet, \n\
consectetur adipiscing elit. Nunc ornare, \n\
diam ultricies vehicula aliquam, mauris \n\
ipsum dapibus dolor, quis fringilla leo ligula non neque";
```

This kind of works. However, as soon as you miss a trailing space, you get a syntax error, which is not easy to spot. While most script agents support this syntax, it's, however, not a part of the EcmaScript specification.

In the times of **EcmaScript for XML (E4X)**, we could assign a pure XML to a string, which opened a way for declarations such as these:

```
var str = <>Lorem ipsum dolor sit amet,
consectetur adipiscing
elit. Nunc ornare </>.toString();
```

Nowadays E4X is deprecated, it's not supported anymore.

Concatenation versus array join

We can also use string concatenation. It may feel clumsy, but it's safe:

```
var str = "Lorem ipsum dolor sit amet, \n" +
 "consectetur adipiscing elit. Nunc ornare,\n" +
 "diam ultricies vehicula aliquam, mauris \n" +
 "ipsum dapibus dolor, quis fringilla leo ligula non neque";
```

You may be surprised, but concatenation is slower than array joining. So the following technique will work faster:

```
var str = [ "Lorem ipsum dolor sit amet, \n",
 "consectetur adipiscing elit. Nunc ornare,\n",
 "diam ultricies vehicula aliquam, mauris \n",
 "ipsum dapibus dolor, quis fringilla leo ligula non neque"].join( ""
);
```

Template literal

What about ES6? The latest EcmaScript specification introduces a new sort of string literal, template literal:

```
var str = `Lorem ipsum dolor sit amet, \n
consectetur adipiscing elit. Nunc ornare, \n
diam ultricies vehicula aliquam, mauris \n
ipsum dapibus dolor, quis fringilla leo ligula non neque`;
```

Now the syntax looks elegant. But there is more. Template literals really remind us of NOWDOC. You can refer any variable declared in the scope within the string:

```
"use strict";
var title = "Some title",
    text = "Some text",
    str = `<div class="message">
<h2>${title}</h2>
<article>${text}</article>
</div>`;
console.log( str );
```

The output is as follows:

```
<div class="message">
<h2>Some title</h2>
<article>Some text</article>
</div>
```

If you wonder when can you safely use this syntax, I have a good news for you — this feature is already supported by (almost) all the major script agents (`http://kangax.github.io/compat-table/es6/`).

Multi-line strings via transpilers

With the advance of ReactJS, Facebook's EcmaScript language extension named JSX (`https://facebook.github.io/jsx/`) is now really gaining momentum. Apparently influenced by previously mentioned E4X, they proposed a kind of string literal for XML-like content without any screening at all. This type supports template interpolation similar to ES6 templates:

```
"use strict";
var Hello = React.createClass({
 render: function() {
   return <div class="message">
<h2>{this.props.title}</h2>
```

```
<article>{this.props.text}</article>
</div>;
 }
});
```

```
React.render(<Hello title="Some title" text="Some text" />, node);
```

Another way to declare multiline strings is by using CommonJS Compiler (`http://dsheiko.github.io/cjsc/`). While resolving the 'require' dependencies, the compiler transforms any content that is not `.js`/`.json` content into a single-line string:

foo.txt

```
Lorem ipsum dolor sit amet,
consectetur adipiscing elit. Nunc ornare,
diam ultricies vehicula aliquam, mauris
ipsum dapibus dolor, quis fringilla leo ligula non neque
```

consumer.js

```
var str = require( "./foo.txt" );
console.log( str );
```

You can find an example of JSX use in *Chapter 6, A Large-Scale JavaScript Application Architecture.*

Manipulating arrays in the ES5 way

Some years ago when the support of ES5 features was poor (EcmaScript 5th edition was finalized in 2009), libraries such as Underscore and Lo-Dash got highly popular as they provided a comprehensive set of utilities to deal with arrays/collections. Today, many developers still use third-party libraries (including jQuery/Zepro) for methods such as `map`, `filter`, `every`, `some`, `reduce`, and `indexOf`, while these are available in the native form of JavaScript. It still depends on how you use such libraries, but it may likely happen that you don't need them anymore. Let's see what we have now in JavaScript.

Array methods in ES5

`Array.prototype.forEach` is probably the most used method of the arrays. That is, it is the native implementation of `_.each`, or for example, of the `$.each` utilities. As parameters, `forEach` expects an `iteratee` callback function and optionally a context in which you want to execute the callback. It passes to the callback function an element value, an index, and the entire array. The same parameter syntax is used for most array manipulation methods. Note that jQuery's `$.each` has the inverted callback parameters order:

```
"use strict";
var data = [ "bar", "foo", "baz", "qux" ];
data.forEach(function( val, inx ){
  console.log( val, inx );
});
```

`Array.prototype.map` produces a new array by transforming the elements of a given array:

```
"use strict";
var data = { bar: "bar bar", foo: "foo foo" },
    // convert key-value array into url-encoded string
    urlEncStr = Object.keys( data ).map(function( key ){
      return key + "=" + window.encodeURIComponent( data[ key ] );
    }).join( "&" );

console.log( urlEncStr ); // bar=bar%20bar&foo=foo%20foo
```

`Array.prototype.filter` returns an array, which consists of given array values that meet the callback's condition:

```
"use strict";
var data = [ "bar", "foo", "", 0 ],
    // remove all falsy elements
    filtered = data.filter(function( item ){
      return !!item;
    });

console.log( filtered ); // ["bar", "foo"]
```

`Array.prototype.reduce`/`Array.prototype.reduceRight` retrieves the product of values in an array. The method expects a callback function and optionally the initial value as arguments. The callback function receive four parameters: the accumulative value, current one, index and original array. So we can, for an instance, increment the accumulative value by the current one (return acc += cur;) and, thus, we will get the sum of array values.

Besides calculating with these methods, we can concatenate string values or arrays:

```
"use strict";
var data = [[ 0, 1 ], [ 2, 3 ], [ 4, 5 ]],
    arr = data.reduce(function( prev, cur ) {
      return prev.concat( cur );
    }),
    arrReverse = data.reduceRight(function( prev, cur ) {
      return prev.concat( cur );
    });

console.log( arr ); //  [0, 1, 2, 3, 4, 5]
console.log( arrReverse ); // [4, 5, 2, 3, 0, 1]
```

`Array.prototype.some` tests whether any (or some) values of a given array meet the callback condition:

```
"use strict";
var bar = [ "bar", "baz", "qux" ],
    foo = [ "foo", "baz", "qux" ],
    /**
     * Check if a given context (this) contains the value
     * @param {*} val
     * @return {Boolean}
     */
    compare = function( val ){
      return this.indexOf( val ) !== -1;
    };

console.log( bar.some( compare, foo ) ); // true
```

In this example, we checked whether any of the bar array values are available in the `foo` array. For testability, we need to pass a reference of the `foo` array into the callback. Here we inject it as context. If we need to pass more references, we would push them in a key-value object.

As you probably noticed, we used in this example `Array.prototype.indexOf`. The method works the same as `String.prototype.indexOf`. This returns an index of the match found or `-1`.

`Array.prototype.every` tests whether every value of a given array meets the callback condition:

```
"use strict";
var bar = [ "bar", "baz" ],
    foo = [ "bar", "baz", "qux" ],
```

```
/**
 * Check if a given context (this) contains the value
 * @param {*} val
 * @return {Boolean}
 */
compare = function( val ){
  return this.indexOf( val ) !== -1;
};
```

```
console.log( bar.every( compare, foo ) ); // true
```

If you are still concerned about support for these methods in a legacy browser as old as IE6-7, you can simply shim them with `https://github.com/es-shims/es5-shim`.

Array methods in ES6

In ES6, we get just a few new methods that look rather like shortcuts over the existing functionality.

`Array.prototype.fill` populates an array with a given value, as follows:

```
"use strict";
var data = Array( 5 );
console.log( data.fill( "bar" ) ); // ["bar", "bar", "bar", "bar",
"bar"]
```

`Array.prototype.includes` explicitly checks whether a given value exists in the array. Well, it is the same as `arr.indexOf( val ) !== -1`, as shown here:

```
"use strict";
var data = [ "bar", "foo", "baz", "qux" ];
console.log( data.includes( "foo" ) );
```

`Array.prototype.find` filters out a single value matching the callback condition. Again, it's what we can get with `Array.prototype.filter`. The only difference is that the filter method returns either an array or a null value. In this case, this returns a single element array, as follows:

```
"use strict";
var data = [ "bar", "fo", "baz", "qux" ],
    match = function( val ){
      return val.length < 3;
    };
console.log( data.find( match ) ); // fo
```

Traversing an object in an elegant, reliable, safe, and fast way

It is a common case when we have a key-value object (let's say options) and need to iterate it. There is an academic way to do this, as shown in the following code:

```
"use strict";
var options = {
    bar: "bar",
    foo: "foo"
    },
    key;
for( key in options ) {
 console.log( key, options[ key] );
}
```

The preceding code outputs the following:

```
bar bar
foo foo
```

Now let's imagine that any of the third-party libraries that you load in the document augments the built-in Object:

```
Object.prototype.baz = "baz";
```

Now when we run our example code, we will get an extra undesired entry:

```
bar bar
foo foo
baz baz
```

The solution to this problem is well known, we have to test the keys with the Object.prototype.hasOwnProperty method:

```
//...
for( key in options ) {
 if ( options.hasOwnProperty( key ) ) {
   console.log( key, options[ key] );
 }
}
```

Iterating the key-value object safely and fast

Let's face the truth—the structure is clumsy and requires optimization (we have to perform the `hasOwnProperty` test on every given key). Luckily, JavaScript has the `Object.keys` method that retrieves all string-valued keys of all enumerable own (non-inherited) properties. This gives us the desired keys as an array that we can iterate, for instance, with `Array.prototype.forEach`:

```
"use strict";
var options = {
    bar: "bar",
    foo: "foo"
    };
Object.keys( options ).forEach(function( key ){
 console.log( key, options[ key] );
});
```

Besides the elegance, we get a better performance this way. In order to see how much we gain, you can run this online test in distinct browsers such as: `http://codepen. io/dsheiko/pen/JdrqXa`.

Enumerating an array-like object

Objects such as `arguments` and `nodeList` (`node.querySelectorAll`, `document. forms`) look like arrays, in fact they are not. Similar to arrays, they have the `length` property and can be iterated in the `for` loop. In the form of objects, they can be traversed in the same way that we previously examined. But they do not have any of the array manipulation methods (`forEach`, `map`, `filter`, `some` and so on). The thing is we can easily convert them into arrays as shown here:

```
"use strict";
var nodes = document.querySelectorAll( "div" ),
    arr = Array.prototype.slice.call( nodes );

arr.forEach(function(i){
 console.log(i);
});
```

The preceding code can be even shorter:

```
arr = [].slice.call( nodes )
```

It's a pretty convenient solution, but looks like a trick. In ES6, we can do the same conversion with a dedicated method:

```
arr = Array.from( nodes );
```

The collections of ES6

ES6 introduces a new type of objects—iterable objects. These are the objects whose elements can be retrieved one at a time. They are quite the same as iterators in other languages. Beside arrays, JavaScript received two new iterable data structures, Set and Map. Set which are a collection of unique values:

```
"use strict";
let foo = new Set();
foo.add( 1 );
foo.add( 1 );
foo.add( 2 );
console.log( Array.from( foo ) ); // [ 1, 2 ]

let foo = new Set(),
    bar = function(){ return "bar"; };
foo.add( bar );
console.log( foo.has( bar ) ); // true
```

The map is similar to a key-value object, but may have arbitrary values for the keys. And this makes a difference. Imagine that we need to write an element wrapper that provides jQuery-like events API. By using the on method, we can pass not only a handler callback function but also a context (this). We bind the given callback to the cb.bind(context) context. This means addEventListener receives a function reference different from the callback. How do we unsubscribe the handler then? We can store the new reference in Map by a key composed from an event name and a callback function reference:

```
"use strict";
/**
 * @class
 * @param {Node} el
 */
let El = function( el ){
 this.el = el;
 this.map = new Map();
};
/**
 * Subscribe a handler on event
 * @param {String} event
 * @param {Function} cb
 * @param {Object} context
 */
El.prototype.on = function( event, cb, context ){
 let handler = cb.bind( context || this );
```

```
  this.map.set( [ event, cb ], handler );
  this.el.addEventListener( event, handler, false );
};
/**
 * Unsubscribe a handler on event
 * @param {String} event
 * @param {Function} cb
 */

El.prototype.off = function( event, cb ){
  let handler = cb.bind( context ),
      key = [ event, handler ];
  if ( this.map.has( key ) ) {
    this.el.removeEventListener( event, this.map.get( key ) );
    this.map.delete( key );
  }
};
```

Any iterable object has methods, `keys`, `values`, and `entries`, where the keys work the same as `Object.keys` and the others return array values and an array of key-value pairs respectively. Now let's see how we can traverse the iterable objects:

```
"use strict";
let map = new Map()
  .set( "bar", "bar" )
  .set( "foo", "foo" ),
    pair;
for ( pair of map ) {
  console.log( pair );
}

// OR
let map = new Map([
    [ "bar", "bar" ],
    [ "foo", "foo" ],
]);
map.forEach(function( value, key ){
  console.log( key, value );
});
```

Iterable objects have manipulation methods such as arrays. So we can use `forEach`. Besides, they can be iterated by `for...in` and `for...of` loops. The first one retrieves indexes and the second, the values.

The most effective way of declaring objects

How do we declare an object in JavaScript? If we need a namespace, we can simply use an object literal. But when we need an object type, we need to think twice about what approach to take, as it affects the maintainability of our object-oriented code.

Classical approach

We can create a constructor function and chain the members to its context:

```
"use strict";
/**
 * @class
 */
var Constructor = function(){
    /**
     * @type {String}
     * @public
     */
    this.bar = "bar";
    /**
     * @public
     * @returns {String}
     */
    this.foo = function() {
     return this.bar;
    };
},
 /** @type Constructor */
 instance = new Constructor();

console.log( instance.foo() ); // bar
console.log( instance instanceof Constructor ); // true
```

We can also assign the members to the constructor prototype. The result will be the same as follows:

```
"use strict";
/**
* @class
*/
var Constructor = function(){},
    instance;
```

```
/**
 * @type {String}
 * @public
 */
Constructor.prototype.bar = "bar";
/**
 * @public
 * @returns {String}
 */
Constructor.prototype.foo = function() {
 return this.bar;
};
/** @type Constructor */
instance = new Constructor();

console.log( instance.foo() ); // bar
console.log( instance instanceof Constructor ); // true
```

In the first case, we have the object structure within the constructor function body mixed with the construction logic. In the second case by repeating `Constructor.prototype`, we violate the **Do Not Repeat Yourself (DRY)** principle.

Approach with the private state

So how can we do it otherwise? We can return an object literal by the constructor function:

```
"use strict";
/**
 * @class
 */
var Constructor = function(){
    /**
     * @type {String}
     * @private
     */
    var baz = "baz";
    return {
      /**
       * @type {String}
       * @public
       */
      bar: "bar",
      /**
```

```
        * @public
        * @returns {String}
        */
        foo: function() {
         return this.bar + " " + baz;
         }
      };
    },
    /** @type Constructor */
    instance = new Constructor();

  console.log( instance.foo() ); // bar baz
  console.log( instance.hasOwnProperty( "baz") ); // false
  console.log( Constructor.prototype.hasOwnProperty( "baz") ); // false
  console.log( instance instanceof Constructor ); // false
```

The advantage of this approach is that any variables declared in the scope of the constructor are in the same closure as the returned object, and therefore, available through the object. We can consider such variables as private members. The bad news is that we will lose the constructor prototype. When a constructor returns an object during instantiation, this object becomes the result of a whole new expression.

Inheritance with the prototype chain

What about inheritance? The classical approach would be to make the subtype prototype an instance of supertype:

```
"use strict";
 /**
  * @class
  */
var SuperType = function(){
      /**
       * @type {String}
       * @public
       */
      this.foo = "foo";
   },
   /**
    * @class
    */
   Constructor = function(){
      /**
       * @type {String}
```

```
    * @public
    */
    this.bar = "bar";
},
/** @type Constructor */
instance;

Constructor.prototype = new SuperType();
Constructor.prototype.constructor = Constructor;

instance = new Constructor();
console.log( instance.bar ); // bar
console.log( instance.foo ); // foo
console.log( instance instanceof Constructor ); // true
console.log( instance instanceof SuperType ); // true
```

You may run into some code, where for instantiation `Object.create` is used instead of the new operator. Here you have to know the difference between the two. `Object.create` takes an object as an argument and creates a new one with the passed object as a prototype. In some ways, this reminds us of cloning. Examine this, you declare an object literal (proto) and create a new object (instance) with `Object.create` based on the first one. Whatever changes you do now on the newly created object, they won't be reflected on the original (proto). But if you change a property of the original, you will find the property changed in its derivative (instance):

```
"use strict";
var proto = {
 bar: "bar",
 foo: "foo"
},
instance = Object.create( proto );
proto.bar = "qux",
instance.foo = "baz";
console.log( instance ); // { foo="baz",  bar="qux"}
console.log( proto ); // { bar="qux",  foo="foo"}
```

Inheriting from prototype with Object.create

In contrast to the new operator, `Object.create` does not invoke the constructor. So when we use it to populate a subtype prototype, we are losing all the logic located in a `supertype` constructor. This way, the `supertype` constructor is never called:

```
// ...
SuperType.prototype.baz = "baz";
Constructor.prototype = Object.create( SuperType.prototype );
```

```
Constructor.prototype.constructor = Constructor;

instance = new Constructor();

console.log( instance.bar ); // bar
console.log( instance.baz ); // baz
console.log( instance.hasOwnProperty( "foo" ) ); // false
console.log( instance instanceof Constructor ); // true
console.log( instance instanceof SuperType ); // true
```

Inheriting from prototype with Object.assign

When looking for an optimal structure, I would like to declare members via an object literal, but still have the link to the prototype. Many third-party projects leverage a custom function (*extend*) that merge the structure object literal into the constructor prototype. Actually, ES6 provides an `Object.assign` native method.
We can use it as follows:

```
"use strict";
   /**
    * @class
    */
var SuperType = function(){
    /**
     * @type {String}
     * @public
     */
    this.foo = "foo";
},
/**
 * @class
 */
Constructor = function(){
    /**
     * @type {String}
     * @public
     */
    this.bar = "bar";
},
/** @type Constructor */
instance;

Object.assign( Constructor.prototype = new SuperType(), {
 baz: "baz"
```

```
    });
    instance = new Constructor();
    console.log( instance.bar ); // bar
    console.log( instance.foo ); // foo
    console.log( instance.baz ); // baz
    console.log( instance instanceof Constructor ); // true
    console.log( instance instanceof SuperType ); // true
```

This looks almost as required, except there is one inconvenience. `Object.assign` simply assigns the values of source objects to the target ones regardless of their type. So if you have a source property with an object (for instance, an `Object` or `Array` instance), the target object receives a reference instead of a value. So you have to reset manually any object properties during initialization.

Approach with ExtendClass

ExtendClass, proposed by Simon Boudrias, is a solution that seems flawless (`https://github.com/SBoudrias/class-extend`). His little library exposes the `Base` constructor with the **extend** static method. We use this method to extend this pseudo-class and any of its derivatives:

```
"use strict";
    /**
     * @class
     */
var SuperType = Base.extend({
    /**
     * @pulic
     * @returns {String}
     */
    foo: function(){ return "foo public"; },
    /**
     * @constructs SuperType
     */
    constructor: function () {}
}),
    /**
     * @class
     */
    Constructor = SuperType.extend({
    /**
     * @pulic
     * @returns {String}
     */
```

```
    bar: function(){ return "bar public"; }
  }, {
    /**
     * @static
     * @returns {String}
     */
    bar: function(){ return "bar static"; }
  }),
  /** @type Constructor */
  instance = new Constructor();

console.log( instance.foo() ); // foo public
console.log( instance.bar() ); // bar public
console.log( Constructor.bar() ); // bar static
console.log( instance instanceof Constructor ); // true
console.log( instance instanceof SuperType ); // true
```

Classes in ES6

TC39 (the EcmaScript working group) is pretty aware of the problem, so the new language specification provides extra syntax to structure object types:

```
"use strict";
class AbstractClass {
 constructor() {
   this.foo = "foo";
 }
}
class ConcreteClass extends AbstractClass {
 constructor() {
   super();
   this.bar = "bar";
 }
 baz() {
   return "baz";
 }
}

let instance = new ConcreteClass();
console.log( instance.bar ); // bar
console.log( instance.foo ); // foo
console.log( instance.baz() ); // baz
console.log( instance instanceof ConcreteClass ); // true
console.log( instance instanceof AbstractClass ); // true
```

The syntax looks class-based, but in fact this a syntactic sugar over existing prototypes. You can check with the type of ConcreteClass, and it will give you *function* because ConcreteClass is a canonical constructor. So we don't need any trick to extend supertypes, no trick to refer the supertype constructor from subtype, and we have a clean readable structure. However, we cannot assign properties the same C-like way as we do now with methods. This is still in discussion for ES7 (https://esdiscuss.org/topic/es7-property-initializers). Besides this, we can declare a class's static methods straight in its body:

```
class Bar {
 static foo() {
   return "static method";
 }
 baz() {
   return "prototype method";
 }
}
let instance = new Bar();
console.log( instance.baz() ); // prototype method
console.log( Bar.foo()) ); // static method
```

Actually, there are many in the JavaScript community who consider the new syntax as a deviation from the prototypical OOP approach. On the other hand, the ES6 classes are backwards compatible with most of the existing code. Subclasses are now supported by the language and no extra libraries are required for inheritance. And what I personally like the most is that this syntax allows us to make the code cleaner and more maintainable.

How to – magic methods in JavaScript

In the PHP world, there are things such as *overloading methods*, which are also known as magic methods (http://www.php.net/manual/en/language.oop5.overloading.php). These methods allow us to set a logic that triggers when a nonexisting property of a method is being accessed or modified. In JavaScript, we control access to properties (value members). Imagine we have a custom collection object. In order to be consistent in the API, we want to have the length property that contains the size of the collection. So we declare a getter (get length), which does the required computation whenever the property is accessed. On attempting to modify the property value, the setter will throw an exception:

```
"use strict";
var bar = {
 /** @type {[Number]} */
 arr: [ 1, 2 ],
```

```
/**
 * Getter
 * @returns {Number}
 */
get length () {
  return this.arr.length;
},
/**
 * Setter
 * @param {*} val
 */
set length ( val ) {
  throw new SyntaxError( "Cannot assign to read only property
'length'" );
 }
};
console.log ( bar.length ); // 2
bar.arr.push( 3 );
console.log ( bar.length ); // 3
bar.length = 10; // SyntaxError: Cannot assign to read only property
'length'
```

If we want to declare getters/setters on an existing object, we can use the following:

```
Object.defineProperty:
"use strict";
var bar = {
 /** @type {[Number]} */
 arr: [ 1, 2 ]
};

Object.defineProperty( bar, "length", {
 /**
  * Getter
  * @returns {Number}
  */
 get: function() {
   return this.arr.length;
 },
 /**
  * Setter
  */
 set: function() {
   throw new SyntaxError( "Cannot assign to read only property
'length'" );
```

```
  }
});
```

```
console.log ( bar.length ); // 2
bar.arr.push( 3 );
console.log ( bar.length ); // 3
bar.length = 10; // SyntaxError: Cannot assign to read only property
'length'
```

`Object.defineProperty` as well as the second parameter of `Object.create` specifies a property configuration (whether it is enumerable, configurable, immutable, and how it can be accessed or modified). So, we can achieve a similar effect by configuring the property as read-only:

```
"use strict";
var bar = {};

Object.defineProperty( bar, "length", {
 /**
  * Data descriptor
  * @type {*}
  */
 value: 0,
 /**
  * Data descriptor
  * @type {Boolean}
  */
 writable: false
});

bar.length = 10; // TypeError: "length" is read-only
```

By the way, if you want to get rid of the property accessor in the object, you can simply remove the property:

```
delete bar.length;
```

Accessors in ES6 classes

Another way by which we can declare accessors is using the ES6 classes:

```
"use strict";
/** @class */
class Bar {
 /** @constructs Bar */
 constructor() {
```

```
   /** @type {[Number]} */
   this.arr = [ 1, 2 ];
 }
 /**
  * Getter
  * @returns {Number}
  */
 get length() {
   return this.arr.length;
 }
 /**
  * Setter
  * @param {Number} val
  */
 set length( val ) {
     throw new SyntaxError( "Cannot assign to read only property
'length'" );
 }
}

let bar = new Bar();
console.log ( bar.length ); // 2
bar.arr.push( 3 );
console.log ( bar.length ); // 3
bar.length = 10; // SyntaxError: Cannot assign to read only property
'length'
```

Besides public properties, we can control access to static ones as well:

```
"use strict";

class Bar {
   /**
    * @static
    * @returns {String}
    */
   static get baz() {
       return "baz";
   }
}

console.log( Bar.baz ); // baz
```

Controlling access to arbitrary properties

All these examples show access control to known properties. However, there might be a case when I want a custom storage with a variadic interface similar to `localStorage`. This must be a storage that has the `getItem` method to retrieve stored values and the `setItem` method to set them. Besides, this must work the same way as when you directly access or set a pseudo-property (`val = storage.aKey` and `storage.aKey = "value"`). These can be achieved by using the ES6 Proxy:

```javascript
"use strict";
/**
 * Custom storage
 */
var myStorage = {
    /** @type {Object} key-value object */
    data: {},
    /**
     * Getter
     * @param {String} key
     * @returns {*}
     */
    getItem: function( key ){
      return this.data[ key ];
    },
    /**
     * Setter
     * @param {String} key
     * @param {*} val
     */
    setItem: function( key, val ){
      this.data[ key ] = val;
    }
  },
  /**
   * Storage proxy
   * @type {Proxy}
   */
  storage = new Proxy( myStorage, {
    /**
     * Proxy getter
     * @param {myStorage} storage
     * @param {String} key
     * @returns {*}
     */
```

```
      get: function ( storage, key ) {
        return storage.getItem( key );
      },
      /**
       * Proxy setter
       * @param {myStorage} storage
       * @param {String} key
       * @param {*} val
       * @returns {void}
       */
      set: function ( storage, key, val ) {
        return storage.setItem( key, val );
    }});

storage.bar = "bar";
console.log( myStorage.getItem( "bar" ) ); // bar
myStorage.setItem( "bar", "baz" );
console.log( storage.bar ); // baz
```

Summary

This chapter gives practices and tricks on how to use the JavaScript core features for the maximum effect. In the next chapter, we will talk about module concepts and we will do a walkthrough on scopes and closures. The next chapter will explain the scope context and the ways to manipulate it.

2
Modular Programming with JavaScript

Engineering in general is all about splitting large tasks into small ones and composing the solutions of these tasks in a system. In software engineering, we break the code-base into modules by following the principles of low coupling and high cohesion. In this chapter, we will talk about the approaches to create modules in JavaScript by covering the following topics:

- How to get out of a mess using modular JavaScript
- How to use asynchronous modules in the browser
- How to use synchronous modules on the server
- JavaScript built-in module system
- Transpiling CommonJS for in-browser use

How to get out of a mess using modular JavaScript

How many digital photos do you have, probably thousands, or more? Just imagine if your image viewer had no capacity to categorize. No albums, no books, no categories, nothing. It would not be of much use, does it? Now let's assume that you have a JavaScript application in a single file and it grows. When it approaches thousand or more than a thousand lines of code, however good your code design is, from a maintainability perspective, it still turns into a useless *pile* like that enormous list of uncategorized photos. Instead of building a monolithic application, we have to write several independent modules that combine together to form an application. Thus, we break a complex problem into simpler tasks.

Modules

So, what is a module? A module encapsulates code intended for a particular functionality. A module also provides an interface declaring what elements the module exposes and requires. A module is often packaged in a single file, which makes it easy to locate and deploy. A well-designed module implies low coupling (the degree of interdependence between modules) and high cohesion (the degree to which the elements of a module belong together).

What are the advantages that modules give us in JavaScript?

Cleaner global scope

You know in JavaScript any assignation that we do out of any function scope makes a new member of the global scope (a built-in object window in a browser or global in Node.js/Io.js). Therefore, we are always at a risk of overriding accidentally an already defined property. On the contrary, whatever is declared in a module stays here unless we explicitly export it.

Packaging code into files

In server-side languages, applications consist of numerous files. One of the best practices here is that a file may contain only one class and have only one responsibility. Besides, a fully-qualified class name must reflect its file location. So when we run into a problem on an object, we can easily deduct where to find its source code. We can divide JavaScript application code into separate scripts, but these will share the same scope and won't give us any encapsulation. Moreover, when the scripts load asynchronously, the internal dependencies must be solved, which is not easy to do. But if we use modules, each is given a dedicated file and has its own scope. A module loader takes care of asynchronous dependencies.

Reuse

Imagine, while working on a project, you wrote a code that solves one task—let's say it provides a convenient API to manage cookies. When switching to another project, you realize that your cookie manager would quite be in place there. In case of *spaghetti code*, you would have to extract the component code, decouple it, and bind it to the new place. If you wrote the component as a decently-designed module, you simply take it and plug it in.

Module patterns

Well, we know that modules help and we want to use them. How do we implement a module in JavaScript? First of all, we need to detach the module code from the global scope. We can only do this by a wrapping module code with a function. A common practice here is to go with **Immediately Invoked Function Expression (IIFE)**:

```
IIFE
(function () {
  "use strict";
   // variable defined inside this scope cannot be accessed from
outside
}());
```

A module must also have access points with the surrounding environment. In the same way as we usually deal with functions, we can pass object references to IIFE as arguments.

```
Import
(function ( $, Backbone ) {
   "use strict";
  // module body
}( jQuery, Backbone ));
```

You may have also seen a pattern where a global object (window) is passed with arguments. This way we do not access the global object directly, but by a reference. There is an opinion that the access by a local reference is faster. That's not completely true. I've prepared a Codepen with some tests at http://codepen.io/dsheiko/pen/yNjEar. It shows me that in Chrome (v45), a local reference is really ~20 percent faster; however, in Firefox (v39), this doesn't make any considerable difference.

You can also run a pattern variation with undefined in the parameter list. A parameter that was not supplied with the arguments has an undefined value. So, we do this trick to ensure that we get the authentic undefined object in the scope even if the global undefined object is overridden.

```
Local References
(function ( window, undefined ) {
   "use strict";
  // module body
}( window ));
```

In order to expose a module element outside its scope, we can simply return an object. The result of the function call can be assigned to an external variable, as shown here:

```
Export
/** @module foo */
var foo = (function () {
  "use strict";
      /**
       * @private
       * @type String
       */
    var bar = "bar",
      /**
       * @type {Object}
       */
      foo = {
        /**
         * @public
         * @type {String}
         */
        baz: "baz",
        /**
         * @public
         * @returns {String}
         */
        qux: function() {
          return "qux";
        }
      };
    return foo;
}());

console.log( foo.baz ); // baz
console.log( foo.qux() ); // qux
```

Augmentation

Sometimes we need to mix things up in a module. For example, we have a module that provides core functionality, and we want to plug-in extensions depending on the context of use. Let's say, I have a module to create objects based on pseudo-class declarations.

Basically, during instantiation it automatically inherits from a specified object and calls the constructor method. In a particular application, I want this to also validate the object interface against a given specification. So, I plug this extension to the base module. How is it done? We pass the reference of the base module to the plugin. The link to the original will be maintained, so we can modify it in the scope of the plugin:

```
/** @module foo */
var foo = (function () {
    "use strict";
        /**
         * @type {Object}
         */
      var foo = {
          /**
           * @public
           * @type {String}
           */
          baz: "baz"
        };
      return foo;
    }()),
    /** @module bar */
    bar = (function( foo ){
      "use strict";
      foo.qux = "qux";
    }( foo || {} ));

console.log( foo.baz ); // baz
console.log( foo.qux ); // qux
```

Module standards

We've just reviewed a few ways to implement modules. However, in practice, we rather follow a standardized API. These have been proved by a huge community, adopted by real-world projects, and recognizable by other developers. The two most important standards that we need to keep in mind are **AMD** and **CommonJS 1.1**, and now we would rather look at at ES6 Module API, which is going to be the next big thing.

CommonJS 1.1 loads modules synchronously. The module body is executed once during the first load and the exported object is cached. It is designed for server-side JavaScript and mostly used in Node.js/Io.js.

AMD loads modules asynchronously. The module body is executed once after the first load and the exported object is also cached. This is designed for in-browser use. AMD requires a script loader. The most popular are RequireJS, curl, lsjs, and Dojo.

Soon, we can expect the script engines to gain native support for JavaScript built-in modules. The ES6 modules take the best of the two worlds. Similar to CommonJS, they have a compact syntax and support for cyclic dependencies, and similar to AMD, the modules load asynchronously and the loading is configurable.

How to use asynchronous modules in the browser

To get a grasp on AMD, we will do a few examples. We will need script loader RequireJS (`http://requirejs.org/docs/download.html`). So you can download it and then address the local version in your HTML or give it an external link to CDN.

First of all, let's see how we can create a module and request it. We place the module in the `foo.js` file. We use the `define()` call to declare the module scope. If we pass an object to this, the object simply gets exported:

foo.js

```
define({
  bar: "bar",
  baz: "baz"
});
```

When we pass a function, it is called and its return value is exported:

foo.js

```
define(function () {
  "use strict";
  // Construction
  return {
    bar: "bar",
    baz: "baz"
  };
});
```

Next to foo.js, we place main.js. This code can be described as follows: call the given callback when all the modules supplied to the first argument (here only foo, which means ./foo.js) are loaded and available.

main.js

```
require( [ "foo" ], function( foo ) {
  "use strict";
  document.writeln( foo.bar );
  document.writeln( foo.baz );
});
```

From the HTML (index.html), first we load RequireJS and then main.js:

index.html

```
<script src="https://cdnjs.cloudflare.com/ajax/libs/require.js/2.1.18/
require.min.js"></script>
<script src="main.js" ></script>
```

Loading scripts synchronously when we have a loader doesn't feel right. However, we can do this with the only script element that, in addition, can be forced to load asynchronously:

index.html

```
<script data-main="./main" async
   src="https://cdnjs.cloudflare.com/ajax/libs/require.js/2.1.18/
require.min.js"></script>
```

With the data-main attribute, we tell the loader what module to load first, whenever the module is ready. As we fire up index.html, we will see the values of the foo module properties that we imported in main.js.

`index.html` outputs the exports of the asynchronously loaded modules:

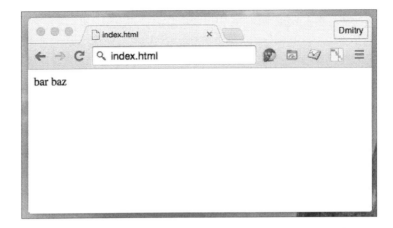

Now we fiddle with more dependencies. So we create the `bar.js` and `baz.js` modules:

bar.js

```
define({
  value: "bar"
});
```

baz.js

```
define({
  value: "baz"
});
```

We have to modify `foo.js` to access these modules:

foo.js

```
define([ "./bar", "./baz" ], function ( bar, baz ) {
  "use strict";
  // Construction
  return {
    bar: bar.value,
    baz: baz.value
  };
});
```

As you may have noticed, the `require`/`define` dependency lists consists of module identifiers. In our case, all the modules and the HTML located in the same directory. Otherwise, we need to build the identifiers based on relative paths (the `.js` file extension can be omitted). If you mess up with a path and RequireJS cannot resolve the dependency, it fires `Error: Script error for:<module-id>`. Not of much help, is it? You can improve error handling on your own. A function expression passed next to the module scope callback receives an exception object as an argument. This object has special properties such as `requireType` (a string containing error types such `timeout`, `nodefine`, `scripterror`) and `requireModules` (an array of module IDs affected by the error).

```
require([ "unexisting-path/foo" ], function ( foo ) {
  "use strict";
  console.log( foo.bar );
  console.log( foo.baz );
}, function (err) {
  console.log( err.requireType );
  console.log( err.requireModules );
});
```

In a well-grained design, modules are numerous and are allocated to a directory tree. In order to avoid relative path computation every time, you can configure the script loader once. So the loader will know where to find the dependency file by a specified alias:

main.js

```
require.config({
    paths: {
        foo: "../../module/foo"
    }
});
require( [ "foo" ], function( foo ) {
  "use strict";
  console.log( foo.bar );
  console.log( foo.baz );
});
```

This gives a bonus. Now if we decided to change a module file name, we do not need to modify every other module that requires it. We just need to change the configuration:

main.js

```
require.config({
  paths: {
```

```
      foo: "../../module/foo-v0_1_1"
    }
});
require( [ "foo" ], function( foo ) {
  "use strict";
  console.log( foo.bar );
  console.log( foo.baz );
});
```

By configuring, we can also address remote modules. For example, here we refer to jQuery, but RequireJS knows the module endpoint from the configuration and, therefore, loads the module from CDN:

require.config({

```
    paths: {
      jquery: "https://code.jquery.com/jquery-2.1.4.min.js"
    }
});

require([ "jquery" ], function ( $ ) {
  // use jQuery
});
```

Pros and cons

The main advantage of the AMD approach is that modules load asynchronously. It also means that while deploying, we don't have to upload the entire code-base, but just a module is changed. And since a browser can handle multiple HTTP requests simultaneously, this way we improve performance. However, here comes a huge trap. It's really quick to load a code in a few separate pieces in parallel. But real-world projects have many more modules. With the HTTP/1.1 protocol, which is still dominant at the moment, loading all of them would take unacceptably long time. Unlike the new standard SPDY and HTTP/2, HTTP/1.1 doesn't cope really well with concurrency during the downloading of a page, and in case of a substantially long queue, this results in head-of-line blocking (`https://http2.github.io/faq/`). RequreJS provides a tool (`http://requirejs.org/docs/optimization.html`) to combine a bunch of modules. This way we don't need to load every single module, but only a few packages. The dependencies packaged together are resolved synchronously. So, one may say that partly we abandon the main benefit of AMD—asynchronous loading. Meanwhile, we must still load a, usually quite heavy, script loader and wrap every single module with the `define()` callback.

From my experience, I would rather advice you to go synchronous with the Common JS modules compiled into packages capable of in-browser use.

How to – use synchronous modules on the server

The following examples require Node.js. It will take just a few minutes to install Node.js using the pre-built installer available at `https://nodejs.org/download/` or even faster via a package manager at `https://github.com/joyent/node/wiki/Installing-Node.js-via-package-manager`.

We will start by putting a simple logic into a module:

foo.js

```
console.log( "I'm running" );
```

Now we can call the module:

main.js

```
require( "./foo" );
```

In order to run the example, we will open the console (under Windows, you can simply run `CMD.EXE`, but I would recommend an enhanced tool like CMDER available at `http://cmder.net/`). In the console, we type the following:

```
node main.js
```

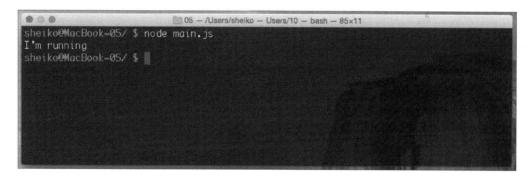

As soon as *Enter* is pressed, the console outputs **I'm running**. So when a module is requested, its body code is invoked. But what if we request the module several times?

main.js

```
require( "./foo" );
require( "./foo" );
require( "./foo" );
```

The result is the same. It outputs **I'm running** only once. This is because the module body code is executed only once when the module is initially requested. An exported object (probably produced by the body code) is cached and acts similar to a singleton:

foo.js

```
var foo = new Date();
```

main.js

```
var first = require( "./foo" ),
    second = require( "./foo" );

console.log( first === second ); // true
```

As you will likely notice, unlike AMD we don't need any wrappers in the modules. But is it still isolated from a global scope?

foo.js

```
var foo = "foo";
```

main.js

```
require( "./foo" );
console.log( typeof foo ); // undefined
```

Any variables defined in a module scope are not available outside the scope. However, if you really want anything to be shared between the module variables behind the exposed interface, you can do it via a global object (Node.js is analogous to an in-browser Windows object).

So what about exports? CommonJS has a preference for single export. We assign to `module.exports` a reference to a type or a value, and this will be the cached return of the required function. If we want multiple exports, we just export an object:

foo.js

```
// module logic
module.exports = {
  bar: "bar",
  baz: "baz"
};
```

main.js

```
var foo = require("./foo");
console.log( foo.bar ); // bar
console.log( foo.baz ); // baz
```

The following is the most common case in Node.js where an object constructor is exported:

foo.js

```
var Foo = function(){
  this.bar = "bar";
}

module.exports = Foo;
```

So through a required call, we receive the constructor function with the prototype and can create instances:

main.js

```
var Foo = require("./foo"),
    foo = new Foo();

console.log( foo.bar ); // bar
```

The same way as we request the foo module from main, we can request from other modules as well:

bar.js

```
// module logic
module.exports = "bar";
```

baz.js

```
// module logic
module.exports = "baz";
```

foo.js

```
// module logic
module.exports = {
  bar: require( "./bar" ),
  baz: require( "./baz" )
};
```

main.js

```
var foo = require( "./foo" );
console.log( foo.bar ); // bar
console.log( foo.baz ); // baz
```

But what if Node.js runs into cyclic dependencies? What if we request back the caller from the called module? Nothing dramatic happens. As you may remember, a module code is executed only once. So if we request `main.js` from `foo.js` after `main.js` is already performed, its body code isn't invoked anymore:

foo.js

```
console.log("Runnnig foo.js");
require("./main");
```

main.js

```
console.log("Runnnig main.js");
require("./foo");
```

When we run `main.js` with Node.js, we get the following output:

```
Runnnig main.js
Runnnig foo.js
```

Pros and cons

CommonJS has a concise and expressive syntax. It's very easy to use. Unit tests are usually written to run in the command line and preferably are a part of continuous integration. A well-designed CommonJS module makes a perfect test unit, which you can access directly from a Node.js-driven test framework (for example, Mocha) far out of the application context. However, CommonJS implies synchronous loading, which is not suitable in a browser. If we want to bypass this limitation, we have to transpile module sources into a single script that resolves module dependencies internally without loading (see "*Traspiling CommonJS for in-browser use*").

UMD

If you want your module to be acceptable both in a browser as AMD and on the server as CommonJS, there is a trick (`https://github.com/umdjs/umd`). By adding a wrapper function, you can dynamically build the export in a desired format depending on the runtime environment.

JavaScript's built-in module system

Well, both AMD and CommonJS are community standards and not a part of the language specification. However, with EcmaScript 6th edition, JavaScript acquired its own module system. At the moment, no browser yet supports this feature, so we have to install the Babel.js transpiler to fiddle with the examples.

Since we already have Node.js that is distributed with NPM (the Node.js package manager), we now can run the following command:

```
npm install babel -g
```

Named exports

Now we can write a module as follows:

foo.es6

```
export let bar = "bar";
export let baz = "baz";
```

In ES6, we can export multiple elements. Any declaration prefixed with the keyword export becomes available for import:

main.es6

```
import { bar, baz } from "./foo";
console.log( bar ); // bar
console.log( baz ); // baz
```

Since we don't yet have any support for ES6 modules in the browser, we will transpile them into CommonJS or AMD. Here Babel.js helps us:

```
babel --modules common *.es6 --out-dir .
```

By this command, we made Babel.js translate all the *.es6 files of the current directory into CommonJS modules. So, we can run the derived main.js module with Node.js:

```
node main.js
```

```
● ● ●                  10 — /Users/sheiko — Users/10 — bash — 85×11
sheiko@MacBook~10/ $ babel --modules common *.es6 --out-dir .
foo.es6 -> foo.js
main.es6 -> main.js
sheiko@MacBook~10/ $ node main.js
bar
baz
sheiko@MacBook~10/ $ 
```

Similarly, we translate ES6 modules to AMD:

```
babel --modules amd *.es6 --out-dir .
```

index.html

```
<script data-main="./main"
  src="https://cdnjs.cloudflare.com/ajax/libs/require.js/2.1.18/
require.min.js"></script>
```

In the previous example, we enlisted our named exports in the import statement. We could also import the entire module and refer to the named exports as properties:

main.es6

```
import * as foo from "./foo";
console.log( foo.bar ); // bar
console.log( foo.baz ); // baz
```

Default export

Besides, we can also do a default export. This is how usually exports are done in Node.js:

foo.es6

```
export default function foo(){ return "foo"; }
```

main.es6

```
import foo from "./foo";
console.log( foo() ); // foo
```

We exported a function and came with the import. This could also be a class or an object.

In AMD, we receive exports as callback arguments, and in CommonJS, as local variables. Though ES6 doesn't export values, but it exports the so called bindings (references) that are immutable. You can read their values, but if you try changing them, you get a type error. Babel.js triggers this error during compilation:

foo.es6

```
export let bar = "bar";
export function setBar( val ) {
    bar = val;
};
```

main.es6

```
import { bar, setBar } from "./foo";
console.log( bar ); // bar
setBar( "baz" );
console.log( bar ); // baz
bar = "qux"; // TypeError
```

The module loader API

In addition to declarative syntax in a separate specification (`https://github.com/whatwg/loader/`), ES6 offers us a programmatic API. It allows us to programmatically work with modules and configure module loading:

```
System.import( "./foo" ).then( foo => {
  console.log( foo );
})
.catch( err => {
  console.error( err );
});
```

Unlike Node.js, the ES6 modules, due to their declarative nature, require imports and exports at the top level. So, this cannot be conditional. However, with the pragmatic loader API, we can do otherwise:

```
Promise.all([ "foo", "bar", "baz" ]
    .map( mod => System.import( mod ) )
  )
  .then(([ foo, bar, baz ]) => {
    console.log( foo, bar, baz );
  });
```

Here we defined a callback that is invoked only when all of the three specified modules are loaded.

Conclusion

Both AMD and CommonJS are interim standards. As soon as the JavaScript built-in module system gets wider support in script engines, we don't really need them anymore. The ES6 modules load asynchronously, and the loading can be configured similar to AMD. They also have a compact and expressive syntax and support for cyclic dependencies similar to CommonJS. In addition, ES provides declarative syntax for static module structure. Such structure can be statically analyzed (static checking, linting, optimization, and so on). ES6 also provides a programmatic loader API. So you can configure how modules are loaded and load modules conditionally. Besides, ES6 modules can be extended with macros and static types.

While everything looks so unclouded, there is still a fly in the ointment. ES6 modules can be pre-loaded synchronously (with `<script type="module"></script>`), but often there is asynchronous loading and this brings us to the same trap as in the case of AMD. Numerous requests over HTTP/1.1 cause a harmful effect on user response time (`https://developer.yahoo.com/performance/rules.html`). On the other hand, SPDY and HTTP/2 that allow multiple requests per TCP connection are getting wider support and eventually will take the place of the dubious HTTP/1.x. Furthermore, W3C works on a standard called *Packaging on the Web* (`https://w3ctag.github.io/packaging-on-the-web/`) that describes how archived files (scripts) can be accepted from a URL (hash). So, we will be able to bundle the entire directory with modules into an archive, deploy, and address them in the same way as we do when we have them in a directory.

Transpiling CommonJS for in-browser use

While HTTP/2 and *Packaging on the Web* are still on their way, we need fast modular applications. As it was previously mentioned, we can divide the application code into CommonJS modules and transpile them for in-browser use. The most popular CommonJS transpiler is surely Browserify (`http://browserify.org`). The initial mission of this tool was to make Node.js modules reusable. They quite succeeded in this. It may feel like magic, but you can really use `EventEmitter` and some other Node.js core modules on the client. However, with the main focus on Node.js compatibility, the tool provides too few options for CommonJS compilation. For example, if you want dependency configuration, you have to use a plugin. In a real-world project, you will likely end up with multiple plugins, where each has a specific configuration syntax. So the setup in general gets over-complicated. Rather, we'll examine here another tool called CommonJS Compiler (`https://github.com/dsheiko/cjsc`). This is a considerably small utility designed to bring CommonJS modules into the browser. The tool is very easy to configure and use, which makes it a good choice to illustrate the concept.

First of all, we install `cjsc`:

```
npm install cjsc -g
```

Now we can take an example from the *How to synchronous modules on the server* section and transpile it for in-browser use:

bar.js

```
// module logic
module.exports = "bar";
```

foo.js

```
// module logic
module.exports = {
  bar: require( "./bar" )};
```

main.js

```
var foo = require( "./foo" );
document.writeln( foo.bar ); // bar
```

The starting point is `main.js`. So, we tell `cjsc` to bundle this module with all the required dependencies recursively into `bundle.js`:

```
cjsc main.js -o bundle.js
```

Let's take a look into the generated file. `cjsc` replaced all the require calls with custom `_require` and put them into the beginning `_require` function definition. This little trick allows you to run the compiled code in a Node.js/Io.js friendly environment such as NW.js, where the `require` function is still needed for local packages. Every module is wrapped in a function scope supplied with module relevant objects (exports and modules) plus global, which is a reference to the global object (`window`).

```
Compiled Code
_require.def( "main.js", function( _require, exports, module, global )
{
  var foo = _require( "foo.js" );
  console.log( foo.bar ); // bar
  console.log( foo.baz ); // baz
    return module;
  });
```

The generated code is a generic JavaScript that we can surely address from the HTML:

index.html

```
<script src="bundle.js"></script>
```

Our sources are still in a CommonJS module. This means that we can access them directly from a Node.js-based framework for unit-testing. The official site for Mocha.js Test is `http://mochajs.org/`:

```
var expect = require( "chai" ).expect;
describe( "Foo module", function(){
  it( "should bypass the export of bar", function(){
      var foo = require( "./foo" );
      expect( foo ).to.have.property( "bar" );
      expect( foo.bar ).to.eql( "bar" );
  });
});
```

`cjsc` has a number of options. But in a real project, typing a long command-line with every build would be annoying and unproductive:

```
cjsc main-module.js -o build.js  --source-map=build/*.map \
--source-map-root=../src -M --banner="/*! pkg v.0.0.1 */"
```

That is why we use task runners such as `Grunt`, `Gulp`, `Cake`, and `Broccoli`. `Grunt` (`http://gruntjs.com`) is the most popular task runner at the moment and has an overwhelming number of plugins available (see the Grunt versus Gulp infographic at `http://sixrevisions.com/web-development/grunt-vs-gulp/`). So, we install the `grunt` command-line interface globally:

```
npm install -g grunt-cli
```

In order to setup a `Grunt` project, we need two configuration files, `package.json` (`https://docs.npmjs.com/files/package.json`) and the `Gruntfile.js` file. The first one contains metadata about NPM packages required to run `Grunt` tasks. The second is needed to define and configure the tasks.

Here we can start with a very minimalistic `package.json` that has only an arbitrary project name and its version in a semver (`http://semver.org/`) format:

package,json

```
{
  "name": "project-name",
  "version": "0.0.1"
}
```

Now we can install the required NPM packages:

```
npm install --save-dev grunt
npm install --save-dev grunt-cjsc
```

Thus we get a local Grunt and a Grunt plugin for CommonJs compiler. The `--save-dev` special option creates `devDependencies` (if it doesn't exist) in the `package.json` section and populates it with the installed dependency. So for instance, when we pull the project sources from a version control system, we can restore all the dependencies by simply running `npm install`.

In `Gruntfile.js`, we have to load the already installed `grunt-cjsc` plugin and configure a task called `cjsc`. In practice, we will need at least two targets that provide different configurations for this task. The first one, `cjsc:debug`, runs `cjsc` to produce uncompressed code, provided with source map. The second one, `cjsc:build` is used to prepare assets for deployment. So we get minified code in `bundle.js`:

Gruntfile.js

```javascript
module.exports = function( grunt ) {
  // Project configuration.
  grunt.initConfig({
    pkg: grunt.file.readJSON( "package.json" ),
    cjsc: {
      // A target to generate uncompressed code with sources maps
      debug: {
        options: {
          sourceMap: "js/*.map",
          sourceMapRoot: "src/",
          minify: false
        },
        files: { "js/bundle.js": "js/src/main.js" }
      },
      // A target to build project for production
      build: {
        options: {
          minify: true,
          banner: "/*! <%= pkg.name %> - v<%= pkg.version %> - " +
          "<%= grunt.template.today(\"yyyy-mm-dd\") %> */"
        },
        files: { "js/bundle.js": "js/src/main.js" }
      }
    }
  });
```

```
// Load the plugin that provides the task.
grunt.loadNpmTasks( "grunt-cjsc" );

// Make it default task
grunt.registerTask( "default", [ "cjsc:build" ] );

};
```

As you can see from the configuration, `cjsc` is intended to transpile `js/src/main.js` into `js/bundle.js`. So we can take the module of the previous example and copy them into `./js/src`.

Now, when we have everything in place, we will run a task. For example, see the following:

grunt cjsc:debug

As mentioned earlier, we can configure dependency mapping with `cjsc`. We just need to describe the dependencies in an object literal that can be supplied to `cjsc` as a JSON-file in the command-line interface or injected into a Grunt configuration:

```
{
  "jquery": {
    "path": "./vendors/jQuery/jquery.js"
  },
  "underscore": {
    "globalProperty": "_"
  },
  "foo": {
    "path": "./vendors/3rdpartyLib/not-a-module.js",
    "exports": [ "notAModule" ],
    "imports": [ "jquery" ]
  }
}
```

Here we declare the `jquery` alias (shortcut) for a module located in `./vendors/jQuery/jqueiry.js`. We also state that a globally exposed `"_"` (Underscore.js) library has to be treated as a module. At the end, we specify the path, exports, and imports for a third-party component. Thus, we get this in the app (without intervention in its code) as a module, though it's not a module:

```
cjsc main.js -o bundle.js --config=cjsc-conig.json
```

Alternatively we can use the following Grunt configuration:

```
grunt.initConfig({
cjsc main.js -o bundle.js --config=cjsc-conig.json
Grunt configuration
grunt.initConfig({
    cjsc: {
      build: {
        options: {
          minify: true,
          config: require( "fs" ).readFileSync( "./cjsc-conig.json" )
        }
      },
        files: { "js/bundle.js": "js/src/main.js" }
      }
  });
```

Bundling ES6 modules for synchronous loading

Well, as we mentioned in the *JavaScript built-in module system* section, ES6 modules are going to be replace the AMD and CommonJS standards. Moreover, we can already write ES6 code and transpile it into ES5 for now. As soon as the support for ES6 across script agents is good enough, we theoretically can use our code as it is. However, what about performance? In fact, we can compile ES6 modules in CommonJS and then bundle them with `cjsc` for in-browser use:

foo.es6

```
export let bar = "bar";
export let baz = "baz";
```

main.es6

```
import { bar, baz } from "./foo";
document.writeln( bar ); // bar
document.writeln( baz ); // baz
```

First, we compile ES6 into CommonJS modules:

```
babel --modules common *.es6 --out-dir .
```

Then, we bundle CommonJS modules into a script suitable for in-browser use:

```
cjsc main.js -o bundle.js -M
```

Summary

Modular programming is a concept closely related to OOP that encourages us to structure code for better maintainability. In particular, JavaScript modules protect global scope from pollution, divide application code into multiple files, and allow the reuse of application components.

The two module API standards that are mostly used at the moment are AMD and CommonJS. The first one that is designed for in-browser use assumes asynchronous loading. The second is synchronous and intended for server-side JavaScript. However, you should know that AMD has a substantial flaw. A well-grained application design with a plenty of modules over HTTP/1.1 may cause a disaster in terms of application performance. This is the major reason why, recently, the practice of transpiling CommonJS modules for in-browser use is on the rise.

Both these APIs shall be considered as interim standards because the upcoming ES6 modules standard is meant to replace them. At the moment, there are no script engines supporting this feature, but there are transpilers (for example, Babel.js) that allows the translation of ES6 modules into CommonJs or AMD.

3
DOM Scripting and AJAX

When it comes to **Document Object Model (DOM)** manipulation and AJAX, the first instinct could be to use jQuery or Zepta. But doesn't it bother you that you load a weighty third-party library for common tasks, when a browser provides everything that you need? Some people pulled in jQuery for cross-browser compatibility. Well, the library is known to fix the *broken DOM API*. This was really helpful when we supported browsers as old as IE7. However, today we hardly need to care about legacy browsers when their usage share is less than 0.1 percent (`http://www.w3schools.com/browsers/browsers_explorer.asp`). Modern browsers are quite consistent in the support of Web API. By and large, cross-browser compatibility is not an issue anymore.

The second and the most common excuse is that the library simplifies the amount of code you have to write to query and manipulate the DOM. It really simplifies the code to some degree, but the drawback is that nowadays we have a generation of developers who don't know JavaScript and Web API, but only jQuery. Many of them cannot solve a simple task without the library and have no idea what actually happens when they call the library methods. Good code means portability and high performance. One can hardly achieve this without a knowledge of native API.

So in this chapter, we will examine the native way of dealing with DOM and AJAX with a focus on high-performance.

This chapter will cover the following topics:

- High-speed DOM operations
- Communication with the server

High-speed DOM operations

In order to deal with the DOM efficiently, we need to understand its nature. The DOM is a tree structure that represents the document that is open in the browser. Every element of the DOM is an object that is called node.

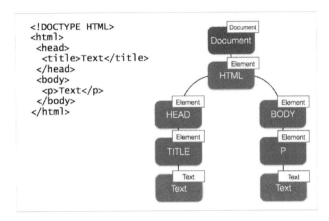

Every node being an object has properties and methods (`https://developer.mozilla.org/en/docs/Web/API/Node`). There are different types of node. In the preceding image, you can see a document node, element nodes, and text nodes. In reality, the tree may also contain specific node types such as comment nodes, doctype nodes, and others. To illustrate the relationships within the tree, we can say that HTML has two child nodes **HEAD** and **BODY**, which relate to each other as siblings. Obviously, HTML is the parent node to HEAD and BODY. We can use these relations that are accessible via node properties to navigate through the tree:

```
var html = document.documentElement;
console.log( html.nodeName ); // HTML

var head = html.childNodes[0];
console.log( head.nodeName );  // HEAD
console.log( head.parentNode === html );  // true
```

This part is clear, but if we request the next sibling to be HEAD instead of BODY. we will get a text node with whitespaces in the content (`nodeValue`):

```
var sibling = head.nextSibling;
// the same as html.childNodes[1]
console.log( sibling.nodeName ); // #text
console.dir( sibling.nodeValue ); // "\n   "
```

In HTML, we usually separate elements with spaces, TABs, and LineFeeds for better readability and these also form a part of DOM. So to access elements, we rather use document and element methods.

Traversing the DOM

Surely you know how to find an element by ID (`document.getElementById`) or by tag name (`document.getElementsByTagName`). You can also search for an element by a CSS selector (`document.querySelector`):

```
<article id="bar">
  <h2>Lorem ipsum</h2>
</article>
var article = document.querySelector( "#bar" ),
    heading = article.querySelector( "h2" );
```

A selector builds from one or many type (tag) selectors, class selectors, ID selectors, attribute selectors, or pseudo-class/element selectors (`http://www.w3.org/TR/CSS21/selector.html%23id-selectors`). Considering the combinations (to match a group, descendants, or siblings), this gives quite a number of possible options. So it can be hard to pick a strategy to bind HTML elements from JavaScript. My advice would be to always use the `data-*` attribute selectors:

```
<article data-bind="bar">
  <h2 data-bind="heading">Lorem ipsum</h2>
</article>

var article = document.querySelector( "[data-bind=\"bar\"]" ),
    heading = article.querySelector( "[data-bind=\"heading\"]" );
```

This way we are independent from the HTML structure. If we change tags, for example for better semantics, nothing breaks on the JavaScript side. We are independent from CSS classes and this means that we can safely refactor CSS. And we are not limited by ID, which is supposed to be unique per document.

While `querySelector` takes the first element in the DOM to match the selector, `querySelectorAll` retrieves all of them:

```
<ul data-bind="bar">
  <li data-bind="item">Lorem ipsum</li>
  <li data-bind="item">Lorem ipsum</li>
  <li data-bind="item">Lorem ipsum</li>
</ul>
```

```
var ul = document.querySelector( "[data-bind=\"bar\"]" ),
      lis = ul.querySelectorAll( "[data-bind=\"item\"]" );
console.log( lis.length );
```

The found elements are represented as a `NodeList`. It looks like an array, but it's not. It's a live collection that is being updated with every DOM reflow. Consider the following example:

```
var divs = document.querySelectorAll( "div" ), i;
for ( i = 0; i < divs.length; i++ ) {
  document.appendChild( document.createElement( "div" ) );
}
```

The preceding code causes an infinite loop, because whenever we access the next element of the collection, one new element is appended to the collection, `divs.length` incremented, and we never meet the loop condition.

It's important to know that an iteration through a live collection (`NodeList`, `HTMLCollection`) is slow and considerably resource-expensive. If you don't need it to be live, just convert the collection into an array such as `[].slice.call( nodeList )`, as covered in *Chapter 1, Diving into JavaScript Core*. In ES6, this can be done with the `[...nodeList]` spread operator:

```
var ul = document.querySelector( "[data-bind=\"bar\"]" ),
      lis = ul.querySelectorAll( "[data-bind=\"item\"]" );
console.log( [].slice.call( lis ) ); // into array ES5 way
console.log( [ ...lis ] ); // into array ES6 way
```

In addition to querying, we can test whether a found element matches a given selector:

```
console.log( el.matches( ".foo > .bar" ) );
console.log( input.matches( ":checked" ) );
```

Changing the DOM

Well, now we know how to find elements in the DOM. Let's see how we can dynamically insert new elements into the DOM tree. There are different ways. We can simply set new HTML content with the `el.innerHTML` method:

```
var target = document.getElementById( "target" );
target.innerHTML = "<div></div>";
```

Otherwise, we can create a node (`document.createElement`) and inject it into the DOM (`el.appendChild`):

```
var target = document.getElementById( "target" ),
    div = document.createElement( "div" ),
target.appendChild( div );
```

Here you should remember that every time we change `el.innerHTML` or append a child to an element, we cause DOM reflow. When this happens repeatedly in a loop, it can slow down the application.

When we pass HTML via `el.innerHTML`, the browser first has to parse the string. It's a resource-consuming operation. However, this will go much faster if we create elements explicitly. If we are producing a batch of similar elements, the flow can be optimized further. Instead of creating every element in a loop, we can clone the one created originally (`el.cloneNode`), which is way faster:

```
var target = document.getElementById( "target" ),
    /**
     * Create a complex element
     * @returns {Node}
     */
    createNewElement = function(){
      var div = document.createElement( "div" ),
          span = document.createElement( "span" );
      span.appendChild( document.createTextNode( "Bar" ) );
      div.appendChild( span );
      return div;
    },
    el;

el = createNewElement();
// loop begins
target.appendChild( el.cloneNode( true ) );
// loop ends
```

On the other hand, we can create a document fragment (`document.createDocumentFragment`) and during the loop append the created nodes to the fragment. Document fragment is a sort of a virtual DOM, which we manipulate instead of the real one. Once we're done, we can inject the document fragment as a branch to the real DOM. By combining this technique and cloning, we are supposed to gain in terms of performance. In effect, this is not certain (`http://codepen.io/dsheiko/pen/vObVOR`). For example, in WebKit browsers, virtual DOM (`document.createDocumentFragment`) runs slower than the real one.

As we've done with performance, let's focus on accuracy. If we need to inject an element to an exact position (for example, between the `foo` and `bar` nodes), `el.appendChild` isn't the right method. We have to go with `el.insertBefore`:

```
parent.insertBefore(el, parent.firstChild);
```

To remove a particular element from the DOM, we do the following trick:

```
el.parentNode.removeChild(el);
```

In addition, we can reload an element, for example, to reset all the subscribed listeners:

```
function reload( el ) {
    var elClone = el.cloneNode( true );
    el.parentNode && el.parentNode.replaceChild( elClone, el );
}
```

Styling the DOM

When it comes to styling, we have to go with CSS classes wherever it is possible. This provides better maintainability—inheritance, composition, and concern separation. You surely know how to assign intended classes to an element via the `el.className` property. However, in the real world, the `el.classList` object is much more useful:

```
el.classList.add( "is-hidden" );
el.classList.remove( "is-hidden" );
var isAvailable = true;
el.classList.toggle("is-hidden", !isAvailable );
if ( el.classList.contains( "is-hidden" ) ){}
```

Here, in addition to the obvious add/remove/contains methods, we also use `toggle`. This method either adds or removes the specified class depending on the Boolean passed as the second argument.

Sometimes we need to manipulate styles explicitly. A part of DOM that is called **CSS Object Model (CSSOM)** provides an interface to manipulate the CSS. Thus, we can read or set dynamic styling information on an element using the `el.style` property:

```
el.style.color = "red";
el.style.fontFamily = "Arial";
el.style.fontSize = "1.2rem";
```

A lesser known technique is to change the actual text of the style rule:

```
el.style.cssText = "color:red;font-family: Arial;font-size: 1.2rem;";
```

As you can see, the second approach is not that flexible. You cannot change or access a single declaration, but only the entire rule. However, styling this way is substantially faster (http://codepen.io/dsheiko/pen/qdvWZj).

While el.style comprises explicit styles of an element, window.getComputedStyle returns inherited (computed) styles:

```
var el = document.querySelector( "h1" ),
    /**
     * window.getComputedStyle
     * @param {HTMLElement} el
     * @param {String} pseudo - pseudo-element selector or null
     * for regular elements
     * @return {CSSStyleDeclaration}
     */
    css = window.getComputedStyle( el, null );
console.log( css.getPropertyValue( "font-family" ) );
```

The cases we've just examined refer to inline styles. In fact, we can access external or internal stylesheets as well:

```
<style type="text/css">
.foo {
 color: red;
}
</style>
<div class="foo">foo</div>
<script type="text/javascript">
var stylesheet = document.styleSheets[ 0 ];
stylesheet.cssRules[ 0 ].style.color = "red";
// or
// stylesheet.cssRules[ 0 ].style.cssText = "color: red;";
</script>
```

Why would we do so? There are special cases. For example, if we want to modify, let's say, pseudo-element style, we have to involve stylesheets:

```
var stylesheet = document.styleSheets[ 0 ];
stylesheet.addRule( ".foo::before", "color: green" );
// or
stylesheet.insertRule( ".foo::before { color: green }", 0 );
```

Making use of attributes and properties

HTML elements have attributes and we can access them from JavaScript:

```
el.setAttribute( "tabindex", "-1" );
if ( el.hasAttribute( "tabindex" ) ) {}
el.getAttribute( "tabindex" );
el.removeAttribute( "tabindex" );
```

While element attributes are defined by HTML, the properties are defined by DOM. And this makes a difference. For example, if you have an input, initially both attribute and property (`el.value`) has the same value. However, when a user or a script changes the value, the attribute is not affected but the property is:

```
// attribute
console.log( input.getAttribute( "value" ) );
// property
console.log( input.value );
```

As you may likely know, in addition to global attributes, there is a special type—custom data attributes. These attributes are meant to provide an exchange of proprietary information between the HTML and its DOM representation, which is used by scripts. The general idea is that you define a custom attribute such as `data-foo` and set a value to it. Then from a script, we access and change the attribute using the `el.dataset` object:

```
console.log( el.dataset.foo );
el.dataset.foo = "foo";
```

If you define a multipart attribute such as `data-foo-bar-baz`, the corresponding `dataset` property will be `fooBarBaz`:

```
console.log( el.dataset.fooBarBaz );
el.dataset.fooBarBaz = "foo-bar-baz";
```

Handling DOM events

Plenty of events happen in the browser. It can be device events (for example, the device changes position or orientation), window events (for example, window size), a process (for example, page loading), media events (for example, video paused), network events (connection status changed), and of course, user interaction events (click, keyboard, mouse, and touch). We can make our code listen to these events and call the subscribed handler functions when the events occur. To subscribe for an event on a DOM element, we use the `addEventListener` method:

```
EventTarget.addEventListener( <event-name>, <callback>, <useCapture>
);
```

In the preceding code, `EventTarget` can be a window, document, an element, or other objects such as `XMLHttpRequest`.

`useCapture` is a Boolean by which you can specify the way you want the event to propagate. For example, a user clicks a button, which is in a form, and we have subscribed handlers to both elements for this click event. When `useCapture` is `true`, the handler of the form element (`ancestor`) will be called first (`capturing flow`). Otherwise, forms handler will be called after the button's handler (`bubbling flow`).

`callback` is a function that is called when an event fires. It receives the `Event` object as an argument, which has the following properties:

- `Event.type`: This is the name of the event
- `Event.target`: This is the event target on which the event occurred
- `Event.currentTarget`: This is the event target to which the listener was attached (`target` and `currentTarget` may differ when we attach the same event handler to multiple elements as mentioned at `https://developer.mozilla.org/en-US/docs/Web/API/Event/currentTarget`)
- `Event.eventPhase`: This indicates which phase of the event flow is being evaluated (none, capturing, at target, or bubbling)
- `Event.bubbles`: This indicates whether or not the event is a bubbling one
- `Event.cancelable`: This indicates whether or not the default action for the event can be prevented
- `Event.timeStamp`: This specifies the event time

Event also has the following methods:

- `Event.stopPropagation()`: This stops further propagation of the event.
- `Event.stopImmediatePropagation()`: If we have multiple listeners subscribed to the same event target, after calling this method none of remaining listeners will be called.
- `Event.preventDefault()`: This prevents the default action. For example, if it's a click event on a button of the submit type, by calling this method we prevent it from submitting the form automatically.

Let's try it now in practice:

```
<form action="/">
<button type="submit">Click me</button>
</form>
<script>
var btn = document.querySelector( "button" )
    onClick = function( e ){
      e.preventDefault();
      console.log( e.target );
    };
btn.addEventListener( "click", onClick, false );
</script>
```

Here, we subscribed an `onClick` listener to a click event on a button element. When the button is clicked, it shows in the JavaScript console the button element that the form isn't submitted.

If we want to subscribe for keyboard events, we can do this as follows:

```
addEventListener( "keydown", function( e ){
    var key = parseInt( e.key || e.keyCode, 10 );
     // Ctrl-Shift-i
    if ( e.ctrlKey && e.shiftKey && key === 73 ) {
      e.preventDefault();
      alert( "Ctrl-Shift-L pressed" );
    }
  }, false );
```

The most common example of process events is the document ready status change. We can listen to the `DOMContentLoaded` or `load` events. The first one is fired when the document has been completely loaded and parsed. The second one also waits for stylesheets, images, and subframes to finish loading. Here, there is a quirk. We have to check `readyState`, because if we register a listener to an event after it has been probably fired, the callback will be never invoked:

```
function ready( cb ) {
  if ( document.readyState !== "loading" ){
    cb();
  } else {
    document.addEventListener( "DOMContentLoaded", cb );
  }
}
```

Well, we know how to subscribe to DOM events with the `EventTarget.`
`addEventListener` method. The `EventTarget` objects also have a method
to unsubscribe from the listeners. For example, see the following:

```
btn.removeEventListener( "click", onClick );
```

If we want to trigger a DOM event, for instance to emulate a button click, we have
to create a new `Event` object, set it up, and dispatch on the element when we want
the event to fire:

```
var btn = document.querySelector( "button" ),
    // Create Event object
    event = document.createEvent( "HTMLEvents" );
// Initialize a custom event that bubbles up and cannot be canceled

event.initEvent( "click", true, false );
// Dispatch the event
btn.dispatchEvent( event );
```

In the same way, we can create our custom event:

```
var btn = document.querySelector( "button" ),
    // Create Event object
    event = document.createEvent( "CustomEvent" );
// Subscribe to the event
btn.addEventListener("my-event", function( e ){
  console.dir( e );
});
// Initialize a custom event that bubbles up and cannot be canceled
event.initEvent( "my-event", true, false );
// Dispatch the event
btn.dispatchEvent( event );
```

Communicating with the server

Many people use third-party libraries to make any request to a server. But do we
need these libraries? Let's examine in the following how AJAX can be used natively
and what will be the next communication API.

XHR

XMLHttpRequest (XHR) is the main API in JavaScript to exchange data between client and server. XHR was firstly presented by Microsoft in IE5 via ActiveX (1999) and had a proprietary syntax in IE browser until version 7 (2006). This led to compatibility issues that called forth the rise of *AJAX-libraries* such as Prototype and jQuery. Today, support for XHR is consistent across all the major browsers. In general, to perform an HTML or HTTPS request, we have to do a number of tasks. We create an instance of XHR, initialize a request via open method, subscribe listeners to request-dependent events, set request headers (`setRequestHeader`), and eventually call the send method:

```
var xhr = new XMLHttpRequest();
xhr.open( "GET", "http://www.telize.com/jsonip?callback=0", true );
xhr.onload = function() {
    if ( this.status === 200 ) {
       return console.log( this.response );
    }
};

xhr.responseType = "json";
xhr.setRequestHeader( "Content-Type", "application/x-www-form-
urlencoded" );
xhr.send( null );
```

More options are available. For example, we can leverage the `progress` and `abort` events to control file uploading (`https://developer.mozilla.org/en-US/docs/Web/API/XMLHttpRequest/Using_XMLHttpRequest`).

It occurs to me that for a simple call, this interface is overcomplicated. There are a plenty of implementations for XHR wrappers on the Internet. One of the most popular implementations can be found at `https://github.com/Raynos/xhr`. It makes the usage of XHR this simple:

```
xhr({
  uri: "http://www.telize.com/jsonip",
  headers: {
    "Content-Type": "application/json"
  }
}, function ( err, resp ) {
  console.log( resp );
})
```

Besides, the library provides a mock object that can be used to replace real XHR in unit tests.

Fetch API

We just examined the XHR API. This looked fine 15 years ago, but now looks clumsy. We have to use wrappers to make it more friendly. Luckily, the language has evolved and nowadays we have a new built-in method called Fetch API. Just consider how easy it is to make a call with it:

```
fetch( "/rest/foo" ).then(function( response ) {
  // Convert to JSON
  return response.json();
}).catch(function( err ) {
  console.error( err );
});
```

In spite of the apparent simplicity, the API is pretty powerful. The `fetch` method expects in the first mandatory argument either a string with a remote method URL or a `Request` object. Request options can be passed in the second optional argument:

```
fetch( "/rest/foo", {
  headers: {
    "Accept": "application/json",
    "Content-Type": "application/json"
  }
});
```

Similar to our previous snippet, the fetch method returns **Promise**. Promises are becoming a common practice for asynchronous or deferred operations. The function called on the Promise-fulfilled event (see then) receives a `Response` object. This function has a number of properties and methods (`https://developer.mozilla.org/en-US/docs/Web/API/Response`). So we can convert the response into JSON, text, blob, or stream with corresponding methods, and we can obtain request-relative information:

```
console.log( response.text() );
console.log( response.status );
console.log( response.statusText );
console.log( response.headers.get( "Content-Type" ) );
```

What about POST requests? Fetch has a mixin called `body` that represents the body of the `Response/Request`. We can pass the POST data through this:

```
var form = document.querySelector( "form[data-bind=foo]" ),
    inputEmail = form.querySelector( "[name=email]" ),
    inputPassword = form.querySelector( "[name=pwd]" );
```

```
fetch( "/feedback/submit", {
  method: "post",
  body: JSON.stringify({
    email: inputEmail.value,
    answer: inputPassword.value
  })
});
```

It accepts not only key-value pairs, but also, for example, `FormData`, so you can submit the whole form including attached files as it is:

```
var form = document.querySelector( "form[data-bind=foo]" );
fetch( "/feedback/submit", {
  method: "post",
  body: new FormData( form )
});
```

At the moment, some of the major browsers (for example, IE/Edge, Safari) don't support this API. However, if you intend to use Fetch API, you can go with the Fetch polyfill (`https://github.com/github/fetch`).

Summary

In the past, every browser's vendors had custom DOM implementations that were largely incompatible. However, this has changed, and we have W3C DOM well supported among browsers at least for a decade. Today, we can safely use JavaScript native API to access, manipulate, and style the DOM.

In JavaScript, XHR is still the main API to communicate between a client and a server. It's not quite developer friendly though. So, we usually write custom wrappers for it.

However, a new API called Fetch is proposed and already implemented in Chrome, Firefox, and Opera. This new API is much easier to use, and compared to XHR, it provides a more impressive and flexible features.

4
HTML5 APIs

While the language specification (**ECMA-262**) changes once in a few years, the new HTML5 APIs sneak in to the language almost with every browser update. The already available APIs are quite numerous. Yet in this chapter, we will focus on those that are used to reconsider the entire development process. We'll learn how we can benefit from multithreading using web workers, how to build an application from reusable independent web components, how to store and search considerably a large amount of data in the client side, and how to establish bidirectional communication with a server.

In this chapter, we will cover the following topics:

- Storing data in a web browser
- Boosting performance with JavaScript workers
- Creating our first web component
- Learning to use server-to-browser communication channels

Storing data in web-browser

Among the HTML5 features, there are a few intended to store data on the client side: Web Storage, IndexedDB, and FileSystem API. We benefit from these technologies when the following happens:

- We want to cache client-side data to make them fetch-able without extra HTTP requests
- We have a significant amount of local data in the web application, and we want our application to work offline

Let's take a look at these technologies.

Web Storage API

In the past, we only had the mechanism to keep the application state, and it was using **HTTP cookies**. Besides unfriendly API, cookies have a few flaws. They generally have a maximum size of about 4 KB. So we simply cannot store any decent amount of data. Cookies don't really fit when the application state is being changed in different tabs. Cookies are vulnerable to **Cross-Site Scripting** attacks.

Now we have an advanced API called **Web Storage**. It provides greater storage capacity (5-25 MB depending on the browser) and doesn't attach any data to the HTTP request headers. There two JavaScript built-in objects implementing this interface: **localStorage** and **sessionStorage**. The first is used as persistent data storage and the second to keep the data during a session.

Storage API is very simple to use, as shown here:

```
var storage = isPersistent ? localStorage : sessionStorage;
storage.setItem( "foo", "Foo" );
console.log( storage.getItem( "foo" ) );
storage.removeItem( "foo" );
```

Alternatively, we can use getters/setters for convenience, as follows:

```
storage.foo = "Foo";
console.log( storage.foo );
delete storage.foo;
```

If we want to iterate through the storage, we can use `storage.length` and `storage.key()`:

```
var i = 0, len = storage.length, key;
for( ; i < len; i++ ) {
  key = storage.key( i );
  storage.getItem( key );
}
```

As you can see, the Web Storage API is much more developer-friendly compared to cookies. It's also more powerful. One of the most common real-life examples where we need storage is the shopping cart. While designing the application, we have to keep in mind that a user, while making their choices, often opens pages with product details in multiple tabs or windows. So we should take care of storage synchronization across all the open pages.

Fortunately, whenever we update the localStorage, the `storage` event is fired on the window object. So we can subscribe a handler for this event to update the shopping cart with the actual data. A simple code illustrating this example may look like this:

```html
<html>
  <head>
    <title>Web Storage</title>
  </head>
  <body>
    <div>
      <button data-bind="btn">Add to cart</button>
      <button data-bind="reset">Reset</button>
    </div>
    <output data-bind="output">

    </output>
    <script>

    var output = document.querySelector( "[data-bind=\"output\"]" ),
        btn = document.querySelector( "[data-bind=\"btn\"]" ),
        reset = document.querySelector( "[data-bind=\"reset\"]" ),
        storage = localStorage,
      /**
       * Read from the storage
       * @return {Arrays}
       */
      get = function(){
          // From the storage we receive either JSON string or null
          return JSON.parse( storage.getItem( "cart" ) ) || [];
      },
      /**
        * Append an item to the cart
        * @param {Object} product
        */
      append = function( product ) {
        var data = get();
        data.push( product );
          // WebStorage accepts simple objects, so we pack the object
into JSON string          storage.setItem( "cart", JSON.stringify( data
) );
        },
        /** Re-render list of items */
```

```
                updateView = function(){
                  var data = get();
                  output.innerHTML = "";
                  data && data.forEach(function( item ){
                    output.innerHTML += [ "id: ", item.id, "<br />" ].join( ""
    );
                  });
                };

        this.btn.addEventListener( "click", function(){
          append({ id: Math.floor(( Math.random() * 100 ) + 1 ) });
          updateView();
        }, false );

        this.reset.addEventListener( "click", function(){
          storage.clear();
          updateView();
        }, false );

        // Update item list when a new item is added in another window/tab
        window.addEventListener( "storage", updateView, false );

        updateView();

        </script>
      </body>
    </html>
```

To see this in action, we have to open the code HTML in two or more tabs. Now when we click the **Add to cart** button, we have a list of the ordered items updated in every tab. As you may have probably noticed, we can also clean up the cart by clicking the **Reset** button. This calls the `storage.clear` method and empties the list. If you want to use sessionStorage here instead of localStorage, I have to warn you that this won't work. The sessionStorage is isolated for every tab or window, so we cannot communicate across them this way.

However, we could have ran this example with sessionStorage if we had the page loaded in a different frame, but on the same window though. Following screenshot is an example of Shopping cart app in action:

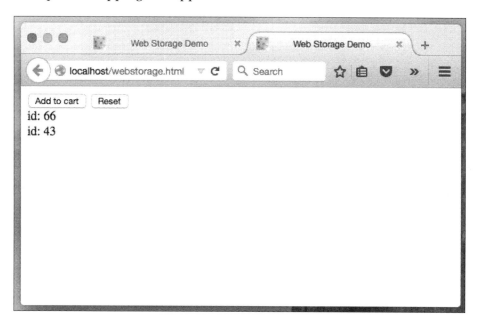

IndexedDB

Web Storage serves well when we have to store a considerably small amount of data (megabytes). However, if we need structured data in a much greater quantity and we want do performance searches through this data using indices, we will use IndexedDB API. The idea of an API to store data in databases in a browser isn't new. A few years ago, Google and their partners were actively advocating a standard candidate called **Web SQL Database**. This specification has failed to make it through W3C recommendation though. Now, we have IndexedDB API instead that is widely-supported already and provides a significant performance boost (asynchronous API and robust search due to indexed keys).

However, the API of IndexedDB is pretty complex. It's also quite hard to read because of a large amount of nested callbacks:

```
/**
 * @type {IDBOpenDBRequest}
 * Syntax: indexedDB.open( DB name, DB version );
 */
var request = indexedDB.open( "Cem", 2 );
```

```
/** Report error */
request.onerror = function() {
  alert( "Opps, something went wrong" );
};
/**
 * Create DB
 * @param {Event} e
 */
request.onupgradeneeded = function ( e ) {
  var objectStore;
  if ( e.oldVersion ) {
    return;
  }
  // define schema
  objectStore = e.currentTarget.result.createObjectStore( "employees",
{ keyPath: "email" });
  objectStore.createIndex( "name", "name", { unique: false } );
   // Populate objectStore with test data
  objectStore.add({ name: "John Dow", email: "john@company.com" });
  objectStore.add({ name: "Don Dow", email: "don@company.com" });
};
/**
 * Find a row from the DB
 * @param {Event} e
 */
request.onsuccess = function( e ) {
  var db = e.target.result,
      req = db.transaction([ "employees" ]).objectStore( "employees"
).get( "don@company.com" );

  req.onsuccess = function() {
    console.log( "Employee matching `don@company.com` is `" + req.
result.name + "`" );
  };
};
```

In this sample, we created a request for opening DB. If the DB doesn't exist or its version is changed, the `upgradeneeded` event is fired. In the function subscribed to this event, we can define the schema by declaring object stores and their indices. So if we need to update the schema of the existing DB, we can increment the version number, `upgradeneeded` will fire again and the listener will be called to update the schema. As soon as we have defined the schema, we can populate the object store with sample data. When the request to open the DB is complete, we request the record that matches the email ID `don@company.com`. When the request is done, we go inside the console:

```
Employee matching 'don@company.com` is `Don Dow'
```

Pretty tangled, isn't it? This API makes me think of a wrapper. The best I know is called **Dexie** (http://www.dexie.org). Just compare how easy it is to solve the same task with the interface it exposes:

```
<script src="./Dexie.js"></script>
<script>
var db = new Dexie( "Cem" );
// Define DB
db.version( 3 )
  .stores({ employees: "name, email" });

// Open the database
db.open().catch(function( err ){
  alert( "Opps, something went wrong: " + err );
});

// Populate objectStore with test data
db.employees.add({ name: "John Dow", email: "john@company.com" });
db.employees.add({ name: "Don Dow", email: "don@company.com" });

// Find an employee by email
db.employees
  .where( "email" )
  .equals( "don@company.com" )
  .each(function( employee ){
    console.log( "Employee matching `don@company.com` is `" +
employee.name + "`" );
  });

</script>
```

FileSystem API

Well, in a web application, we can store key value pairs with Web Storage and we can create and use IndexedDB. Something is still missing. Desktop applications can read and write files and directories. That is what we often need in a web application that is capable of running offline. The FileSystem API allows us to create, read, and write to a user's local file system in application scope. Let's take up an example:

```
window.requestFileSystem  = window.requestFileSystem || window.
webkitRequestFileSystem;
    /**
      * Read file from a given FileSystem
      * @param {DOMFileSystem} fs
```

```
          * @param {String} file
          */
     var readFile = function( fs, file ) {
          console.log( "Reading file " + file );
          // Obtain FileEntry object
          fs.root.getFile( file, {}, function( fileEntry ) {
            fileEntry.file(function( file ){
                // Create FileReader
                var reader = new FileReader();
                reader.onloadend = function() {
                  console.log( "Fetched content: ", this.result );
                };
                // Read file
                reader.readAsText( file );
            }, console.error );
          }, console.error );
     },
     /**
       * Save file into a given FileSystem and run onDone when ready
       * @param {DOMFileSystem} fs
       * @param {String} file
       * @param {Function} onDone
       */
     saveFile = function( fs, file, onDone ) {
        console.log( "Writing file " + file );
        // Obtain FileEntry object
        fs.root.getFile( file, { create: true }, function( fileEntry ) {
          // Create a FileWriter object for the FileEntry
          fileEntry.createWriter(function( fileWriter ) {
            var blob;
            fileWriter.onwriteend = onDone;
            fileWriter.onerror = function(e) {
              console.error( "Writing error: " + e.toString() );
            };
            // Create a new Blob out of the text we want into the file.
            blob = new Blob([ "Lorem Ipsum" ], { type: "text/plain" });
            // Write into the file
            fileWriter.write( blob );
          }, console.error );
        }, console.error );
     },
     /**
       * Run when FileSystem initialized
       * @param {DOMFileSystem} fs
       */
```

```
onInitFs = function ( fs ) {
  const FILENAME = "log.txt";
  console.log( "Opening file system: " + fs.name );
  saveFile( fs, FILENAME, function(){
    readFile( fs, FILENAME );
  });
};
```

```
window.requestFileSystem( window.TEMPORARY, 5*1024*1024 /*5MB*/,
onInitFs, console.error );
```

First of all, we request for a local file system (`requestFileSystem`) that's sandboxed to the application. With the first argument, we state whether the file system should be persistent. By passing `window.TEMPORARY` in the argument, we allow the browser to remove the data automatically (for example, when more space is needed). If we go with `window.PERSISTENT`, we determine that the data cannot be cleaned without explicit user confirmation. The second argument specifies how much space we can allocate for the file system. Then, there are the `onSuccess` and `onError` callbacks. When the file system is created, we receive a reference to the `FileSystem` object. This object has the `fs.root` property, where the object keeps `DirectoryEntry` bound to the root file system directory. The `DirectoryEntry` object has the `DirectoryEntry.getDirectory`, `DirectoryEntry.getFile`, `DirectoryEntry.removeRecursevly`, and `DirectoryEntry.createReader` methods. In the preceding example, we write into the current (`root`) directory, so we simply use `DirectoryEntry.getFile` to open a file of a given name. On successfully opening a file, we receive `FileEntry` that represents the open file. The object has a few properties such as: `FileEntry.fullPath`, `FileEntry.isDirectory`, `FileEntry.isFile`, and `FileEntry.name` and methods such as `FileEntry.file` and `FileEntry.createWriter`. The first method returns the `File` object, which can be used to read file content, and the second is used to write in the file. By the time the operation is complete, we read from the file. For this, we create a `FileReader` object and make it read our `File` object as text.

Boosting performance with JavaScript workers

JavaScript is a single-threaded environment. So, multiple scripts cannot really run simultaneously. Yes, we use `setTimeout()`, `setInterval()`, `XMLHttpRequest` and event handlers to run tasks asynchronously. So we gain non-blocking execution, but this doesn't mean concurrency. However, using web workers, we can run one or more scripts in the background independent of the UI scripts. Web workers are long running scripts that are not interrupted by blocking UI events. Web workers utilize multithreading, so we can benefit from multicore CPUs.

Well, where can we use web workers? Anywhere where we do processor-intensive calculations and don't want them blocking the UI thread. It can be graphics, web games, crypto, and Web I/O. We cannot manipulate the DOM from a web worker directly, but we have access to XMLHttpRequest, Web Storage, IndexedDB, FileSystem API, Web Sockets and other features.

So let's see what these web workers are in practice. By and large, we register an existing web worker in the main script and communicate to the web worker using the PostMessage API (https://developer.mozilla.org/en-US/docs/Web/API/Window/postMessage):

```
index.html
<html>
  <body>
<script>
"use strict";
// Register worker
var worker = new Worker( "./foo-worker.js" );
// Subscribe for worker messages
worker.addEventListener( "message", function( e ) {
  console.log( "Result: ", e.data );
}, false );
console.log( "Starting the task..." );
// Send a message to worker
worker.postMessage({
  command: "loadCpu",
  value: 2000
});
</script>
  </body>
</html>
foo-worker.js
"use strict";
var commands = {
  /**
   * Emulate resource-consuming operation
   * @param {Number} delay in ms
   */
  loadCpu: function( delay ) {
    var start = Date.now();
    while (( Date.now() - start ) < delay );
    return "done";
  }
};
```

```
// Workers don't have access to the window object.
// To access global object we have to use self object instead.
self.addEventListener( "message", function( e ) {
  var command;
  if ( commands.hasOwnProperty( e.data.command ) ) {
    command = commands[ e.data.command ];
    return self.postMessage( command( e.data.value ) );
  }
  self.postMessage( "Error: Command not found" );

}, false );
```

Here in `index.html`, we requested the web worker (`foo-worker.js`) to subscribe for worker messages and requested it to load the CPU for 2,000 ms, which represents a resource-consuming process. The worker receives the message and checks for a function specified in the `command` property. If this exists, the workers pass the message value to the function and replies with the return value.

Note that despite of launching such an expensive process by starting up `index.html`, the main thread stays nonblocked. Nonetheless, it reports to the console when the process is complete. But if you try to run the `loadCpu` function within the main script, the UI freezes and most probably results in a script-timeout error. Now consider this: if you call `loadCpu` asynchronously (for instance, with `setTimeout`), the UI will still hang. The only safe way to deal with processor-sensitive operations is to hand them over to web workers.

Web workers can be dedicated and shared. A dedicated worker is accessible only through a script, the one where we call the worker. Shared workers can be accessed from multiple scripts, even those running in different windows. That makes this API a bit different:

index.html

```
<script>
"use strict";
var worker = new SharedWorker( "bar-worker.js" );
worker.port.onmessage = function( e ) {
  console.log( "Worker echoes: ", e.data );
};
worker.onerror = function( e ){
  console.error( "Error:", e.message );
};
worker.port.postMessage( "Hello worker" );
</script>
bar-worker.js
"use strict";
```

```
onconnect = function( e ) {
  var port = e.ports[ 0 ];
  port.onmessage = function( e ) {
    port.postMessage( e.data );
  };
  port.start();
};
```

The preceding example worker simply echoes the received message. If the worker does some effective computation, we would be able to command it from different scripts on different pages.

These examples show the use of web workers for concurrent computations. What about unloading the main thread from some of the web I/O operations? For example, we are requested to report specified UI events to a remote **Business Intelligence Server (BI Server** is used here to receive statistical data). This is not a core functionality, so it would be great to keep any loads that these requests produce out of the main thread. So we can use a web worker. However, a worker is available only after it's loaded. Normally, this happens very fast, but I still want to be sure that no BI events are lost because the worker was unavailable. What I can do is embed the web worker code into HTML and register the web worker by data URI:

```
<script data-bind="biTracker" type="text/js-worker">
  "use strict";

  // Here shall go you BI endpoint
  const REST_METHOD = "http://www.telize.com/jsonip";
  /**
   * @param {Map} data - BI request params
   * @param {Function} resolve
   */
  var call = function( data, resolve ) {
    var xhr = new XMLHttpRequest(),
        params = data ? Object.keys( data ).map(function( key ){
            return key + "=" + encodeURIComponent( data[ key ] );
          }).join( "&" ) : "";

    xhr.open( "POST", REST_METHOD, true );
    xhr.addEventListener( "load", function() {
        if ( this.status >= 200 && this.status < 400 ) {
          return resolve( this.response );
        }
        console.error( "BI tracker - bad request " + this.status );
      }, false );
```

```
      xhr.addEventListener( "error", console.error, false );
      xhr.responseType = "json";
      xhr.setRequestHeader( "Content-Type", "application/x-www-form-
  urlencoded" );
      xhr.send( params );
    };
    /**
     * Subscribe to window.onmessage event
     */
    onmessage = function ( e ) {
      call( e.data, function( data ){
        // respond back
        postMessage( data );
      })
    };
</script>

<script type="text/javascript">
  "use strict";
  window.biTracker = (function(){
    var blob = new Blob([ document.querySelector( "[data-
bind=\"biTracker\"]" ).textContent ], {
          type: "text/javascript"
        }),
        worker = new Worker( window.URL.createObjectURL( blob ) );

    worker.onmessage = function ( oEvent ) {
      console.info( "Bi-Tracker responds: ", oEvent.data );
    };
    return worker;
  }());
  // Let's test it
  window.biTracker.postMessage({ page: "#main" });
</script>
```

By handing over the web I/O to a worker, we can also get additional control over it. For example, in reaction to a network status change (the ononline and onoffline events, and the navigator.online property being available to workers), we can respond to an application either with the actual call results or cached ones. In other words, we can make our application work offline. In fact, there are special types of JavaScript workers called Service Workers. Service Workers inherit from Shared Workers and act as a proxy between the web application and the network (https://developer.mozilla.org/en-US/docs/Mozilla/Projects/Social_API/Service_worker_API_reference).

Creating the first web component

You might be familiar with HTML5 video element (http://www.w3.org/TR/html5/embedded-content-0.html#the-video-element). By placing a single element in your HTML, you will get a widget that runs a video. This element accepts a number of attributes to set up the player. If you want to enhance this, you can use its public API and subscribe listeners on its events (http://www.w3.org/2010/05/video/mediaevents.html). So, we reuse this element whenever we need a player and only customize it for project-relevant look and feel. If only we had enough of these elements to pick every time we needed a widget on a page. However, this is not the right way to include any widget that we may need in an HTML specification. However, the API to create custom elements, such as video, is already there. We can really define an element, package the compounds (JavaScript, HTML, CSS, images, and so on), and then just link it from the consuming HTML. In other words, we can create an independent and reusable web component, which we then use by placing the corresponding custom element (<my-widget />) in our HTML. We can restyle the element, and if needed, we can utilize the element API and events. For example, if you need a date picker, you can take an existing web component, let's say the one available at http://component.kitchen/components/x-tag/datepicker. All that we have to do is download the component sources (for example, using the browser package manager) and link to the component from our HTML code:

```
<link rel="import" href="bower_components/x-tag-datepicker/src/datepicker.js">
```

Declare the component in the HTML code:

```
<x-datepicker name="2012-02-02"></x-datepicker>
```

This is supposed to go smoothly in the latest versions of Chrome, but this won't probably work in other browsers. Running a web component requires a number of new technologies to be unlocked in a client browser, such as **Custom Elements**, **HTML Imports**, **Shadow DOM**, and templates. The templates include the JavaScript templates that we examined in *Chapter 1, Diving into JavaScript core*. The Custom Element API allows us to define new HTML elements, their behavior, and properties. The Shadow DOM encapsulates a DOM subtree required by a custom element. And support of HTML imports assumes that by a given link the user-agent enables a web-component by including its HTML on a page. We can use a polyfill (http://webcomponents.org/) to ensure support for all of the required technologies in all the major browsers:

```
<script src="./bower_components/webcomponentsjs/webcomponents.min.js"></script>
```

Do you fancy writing your own web components? Let's do it. Our component acts
similar to HTML's details/summary. When one clicks on **summary**, the details
show up. So we create x-details.html, where we put component styles and
JavaScript with the component API:

x-details.html

```
<style>
  .x-details-summary {
    font-weight: bold;
    cursor: pointer;
  }
  .x-details-details {
    transition: opacity 0.2s ease-in-out, transform 0.2s ease-in-out;
    transform-origin: top left;
  }
  .x-details-hidden {
    opacity: 0;
    transform: scaleY(0);
  }
</style>
<script>
"use strict";
    /**
     * Object constructor representing x-details element
     * @param {Node} el
     */
var DetailsView = function( el ){
      this.el = el;
      this.initialize();
    },
    // Creates an object based in the HTML Element prototype
    element = Object.create( HTMLElement.prototype );
/** @lend DetailsView.prototype */
Object.assign( DetailsView.prototype, {
  /**
   * @constracts DetailsView
   */
  initialize: function(){
    this.summary = this.renderSummary();
    this.details = this.renderDetails();
    this.summary.addEventListener( "click", this.onClick.bind( this ),
false );
    this.el.textContent = "";
    this.el.appendChild( this.summary );
```

```
      this.el.appendChild( this.details );
  },
  /**
   * Render summary element
   */
  renderSummary: function(){
    var div = document.createElement( "a" );
    div.className = "x-details-summary";
    div.textContent = this.el.dataset.summary;
    return div;
  },
  /**
   * Render details element
   */
  renderDetails: function(){
    var div = document.createElement( "div" );
    div.className = "x-details-details x-details-hidden";
    div.textContent = this.el.textContent;
    return div;
  },
  /**
   * Handle summary on click
   * @param {Event} e
   */
  onClick: function( e ){
    e.preventDefault();
    if ( this.details.classList.contains( "x-details-hidden" ) ) {
      return this.open();
    }
    this.close();
  },
  /**
   * Open details
   */
  open: function(){
    this.details.classList.toggle( "x-details-hidden", false );
  },
  /**
   * Close details
   */
  close: function(){
    this.details.classList.toggle( "x-details-hidden", true );
  }
});
```

```
// Fires when an instance of the element is created
element.createdCallback = function() {
  this.detailsView = new DetailsView( this );
};
// Expose method open
element.open = function(){
  this.detailsView.open();
};
// Expose method close
element.close = function(){
  this.detailsView.close();
};
// Register the custom element
document.registerElement( "x-details", {
  prototype: element
});
</script>
```

Further in the JavaScript code, we create an element based on a generic HTML element (`Object.create( HTMLElement.prototype )`). Here we could inherit from a complex element (for example, video) if needed. We register a `x-details` custom element using the earlier one created as a prototype. With `element.createdCallback`, we subscribe a handler that will be called when a custom element is created. Here we attach our view to the element to enhance it with the functionality that we intend for it. Now we can use the component in HTML, as follows:

```
<!DOCTYPE html>
<html>
  <head>
    <title>X-DETAILS</title>
    <!-- Importing Web Component's Polyfill -->
    <!-- uncomment for non-Chrome browsers
    script src="./bower_components/webcomponentsjs/webcomponents.min.
js"></script-->
    <!-- Importing Custom Elements -->
  <link rel="import" href="./x-details.html">
  </head>
  <body>
    <x-details data-summary="Click me">
      Nunc iaculis ac erat eu porttitor. Curabitur facilisis ligula
et urna egestas mollis. Aliquam eget consequat tellus. Sed ullamcorper
ante est. In tortor lectus, ultrices vel ipsum eget, ultricies
facilisis nisl. Suspendisse porttitor blandit arcu et imperdiet.
    </x-details>
  </body>
</html>
```

X-details web-component in action is shown in the following screenshot:

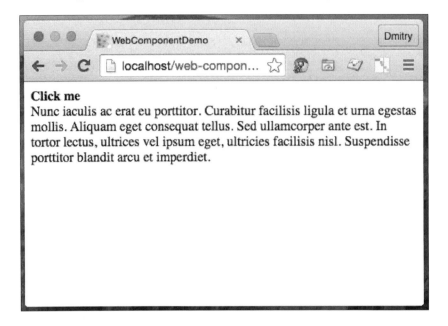

Learning to use server-to-browser communication channels

Using XHR or Fetch API, we can request a state from the server. This is a one-way communication. If we want real-time communication, we need this in the opposite direction as well. For example, we may want user notifications (your post has been liked, new comment, or new private message) to pop up as soon as the corresponding records change in the DB. The server side has connection to the DB, so we expect the server to notify the client. In the past, to receive these events on the client, we were using tricks that were known under the umbrella term **COMET** (hidden iframe, long polling, tag long polling, and others). Now we can go with native JavaScript APIs.

Server-Sent Events

The technology that provides a way to subscribe to server-side events is the **Server-Sent Events (SSE)** API. On the client, we register a server stream (EventSource) and subscribe to the event coming from it:

```
var src = new EventSource( "./sse-server.php" );

src.addEventListener( "open", function() {
   console.log( "Connection opened" );
}, false);

src.addEventListener( "error", function( e ) {
  if ( e.readyState === EventSource.CLOSED ) {
    console.error( "Connection closed" );
  }
}, false );

src.addEventListener( "foo", function( e ) {
  var data = JSON.parse( e.data );
  console.log( "Received from the server:", data );
}, false);
```

Here, we subscribed a listener to a specific event called "foo". If you want your callback to be invoked on every server event, just use src.onmessage. As for the server side, we just need to set the MIME type text/event-stream and send event payload blocks separated with pairs of new lines:

```
event: foo\n
data: { time: "date" }\n\n
```

SSE works via an HTTP connection, so we need a web server to create a stream. PHP is considerably simpler and a widely used server-side language. Chances are that you are already familiar with its syntax. On the other hand, PHP isn't designed for a persistent connection of long duration. Yet, we can trick it by declaring a loop that makes our PHP script never ending:

```
<?PHP
set_time_limit( 0 );
header("Content-Type: text/event-stream");
header("Cache-Control: no-cache");
date_default_timezone_set("Europe/Berlin");
```

```
function postMessage($event, $data){
  echo "event: {$event}", PHP_EOL;
  echo "data: ", json_encode($data, true), PHP_EOL, PHP_EOL;
  ob_end_flush();
  flush();
}
while (true) {
  postMessage("foo", array("time" => date("r")) );
  sleep(1);
}
```

You may have seen SSE examples where the server script outputs the data once and terminates the process (for example, `http://www.html5rocks.com/en/tutorials/eventsource/basics/`). That is also a working example, because every time the connection is terminated by the server, the browser renews the connection. However, this way we do not have any benefit of SSE that works the same as polling.

Now everything looks ready, so we can run the HTML code. As we do this, we get the following output in the console:

```
Connection opened
Received from the server: Object { time="Tue, 25 Aug 2015 10:31:54
+0200"}
Received from the server: Object { time="Tue, 25 Aug 2015 10:31:55
+0200"}
Received from the server: Object { time="Tue, 25 Aug 2015 10:31:56
+0200"}
Received from the server: Object { time="Tue, 25 Aug 2015 10:31:57
+0200"}
Received from the server: Object { time="Tue, 25 Aug 2015 10:31:58
+0200"}
Received from the server: Object { time="Tue, 25 Aug 2015 10:31:59
+0200"}
Received from the server: Object { time="Tue, 25 Aug 2015 10:32:00
+0200"}
Received from the server: Object { time="Tue, 25 Aug 2015 10:32:01
+0200"}
Received from the server: Object { time="Tue, 25 Aug 2015 10:32:02
+0200"}
...
```

Web Sockets

Well, with XHR/Fetch we communicate from client to server. With SSE, we do this in the opposite direction. But can we have communication both ways at once? Another HTML5 goody called Web Sockets provides bidirectional, full-duplex client-server communications.

The client side looks similar to SEE. We just register the Web Socket server, subscribe to its events, and send to it our events:

```
var rtm = new WebSocket("ws://echo.websocket.org");
rtm.onopen = function(){
  console.log( "Connection established" );
  rtm.send("hello");
};
rtm.onclose = function(){
  console.log( "Connection closed" );
};
rtm.onmessage = function( e ){
  console.log( "Received:", e.data );
};
rtm.onerror = function( e ){
  console.error( "Error: " + e.message );
};
```

This demo source at `ws://echo.websocket.org` simply echoes any messages sent to it:

```
Connection established
Received: hello
```

Need something more practical? I believe the most illustrative case would be a chat:

demo.html

```
<style>
  input {
    border-radius: 5px;
    display: block;
    font-size: 14px;
    border: 1px solid grey;
    margin: 3px 0;
  }
  button {
    border-radius: 5px;
    font-size: 14px;
    background: #189ac4;
```

```
      color: white;
      border: none;
      padding: 3px 14px;
    }
</style>

<form data-bind="chat">
  <input data-bind="whoami" placeholder="Enter your name">
  <input data-bind="text" placeholder="Enter your msg" />
  <button type="submit">Send</button>
</form>
<h3>Chat:</h3>
<output data-bind="output">
</output>
<script>

var whoami = document.querySelector( "[data-bind=\"whoami\"]" ),
    text = document.querySelector( "[data-bind=\"text\"]" ),
    chat = document.querySelector( "[data-bind=\"chat\"]" ),
    output = document.querySelector( "[data-bind=\"output\"]" ),
    // create ws connection
    rtm = new WebSocket("ws://localhost:8001");

rtm.onmessage = function( e ){
  var data = JSON.parse( e.data );
  output.innerHTML += data.whoami + " says: " + data.text + "<br />";
};
rtm.onerror = function( e ){
  console.error( "Error: " + e.message );
};

chat.addEventListener( "submit", function( e ){
  e.preventDefault();
  if ( !whoami.value ) {
    return alert( "You have enter your name" );
  }
  if ( !text.value ) {
    return alert( "You have enter some text" );
  }
  rtm.send(JSON.stringify({
    whoami: whoami.value,
    text: text.value
  }));
});

</script>
```

Here we have a form with two input fields. The first expects a person's name and the second, the chat message. When the form is submitted, the values of both inputs are sent to the Web Socket server. Server response is displayed in the output element. Unlike SSE, Web Sockets require a special protocol and server implementation to get working. To run the example, we will take a simple nodejs-based server implementation, **nodejs-websocket** (https://github.com/sitegui/nodejs-websocket):

ws.js

```
        /** @type {module:nodejs-websocket} */
    var ws = require( "nodejs-websocket" ),
        /** @type {Server} */
        server = ws.createServer(function( conn ) {
            conn.on( "text", function ( str ) {
              console.log( "Received " + str );
              broadcast( str );
            });
        }).listen( 8001 ),
        /**
         * Broadcast message
         * @param {String} msg
         */
        broadcast = function ( msg ) {
          server.connections.forEach(function ( conn ) {
            conn.sendText( msg );
          });
        };
```

The script creates a server available on the port 8001 that listens to the Web Socket messages, and when any message is received, the port broadcasts it to all the available connections. We can fire up the server like this:

```
node ws.js
```

Now we open our demo chat in two different browsers. When we send a message from one of them, the message shows up in both browsers. Following screenshot shows the WebSocket-driven chat in Firefox:

Following screenshot shows the WebSocket-driven chat in Chrome:

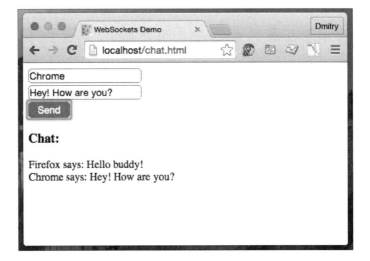

Note how fast the clients react to the events. Communication through sockets gives irrefutable advantages.

There are a number of Web Socket server implementations for various languages, for example, Socket.IO (`http://socket.io`) for Node.js, Jetty (`http://www.eclipse.org/jetty`) for Java, Faye (`http://faye.jcoglan.com`) for Ruby, Tornado (`http://www.tornadoweb.org`) for Python, and even one for PHP called Ratchet (`http://socketo.me`). However, I would like to draw your attention to a language-agnostic WebSocket daemon—Websocketd (`http://websocketd.com/`). It's like **Common Gateway Interface (CGI)**, but for Web Sockets. so you can write the server login in your favorite language and then attach your script to the daemon:

```
websocketd --port=8001 my-script
```

Summary

HTML5 provide a number of awesome APIs, and we just examined some of them. Among browser storage APIs, there are localStorage and sessionStorage that extend the cookies relict. Both are capable of storing megabytes of data and can be easily synchronized across different browser windows/tabs. IndexedDB allows us to store even greater quantity of data and provides an interface for high-performance searches using indices. We can also use FileSystem API to create and operate a local file system bound to the web application.

While JavaScript is a single-threaded environment, we can still run scripts in multiple threads. We can register dedicated or shared Web Workers and hand over any processor-intensive operations, leaving the main thread and the UI unaffected. We also can leverage a special kind of JavaScript workers—Service Workers--- as a proxy between the web application and the network. This enables control to network I/O when the browsers switches mode online/offline.

Nowadays we can create own custom advanced elements that can be easily reused, restyled, and enhanced. The assets required to render such elements are HTML, CSS, JavaScript, and images are bundled as Web Components. So, we literally can build the Web now from the components similar to how buildings are made from bricks.

In the past, we used tricks known as COMET to exchange events between server and client. Now we can use SSE API to subscribe for server events sent over HTTP. We can also use Web Sockets for bidirectional, full-duplex client-server communications.

5
Asynchronous JavaScript

Nowadays Internet users are impatient, a lag of 2-3 seconds during page loading or navigation and they lose their interest and will likely leave the service for something else. Our highest priority is to reduce user response time. The main approach here is known as *Cutting the mustard* (`http://www.creativebloq.com/web-design/ responsive-web-design-tips-bbc-news-9134667`). We extract the components of an application required for core experience and load them first. Then, progressively we add an enhanced experience. As for JavaScript, what we have to care the most about are nonblocking flows. Thus, we have to avoid loading scripts synchronously prior to HTML rendering, and we have to wrap all long-running tasks into asynchronous callbacks. This is something that you most probably already know. But do you do it efficiently?

In this chapter, we will cover the following topics:

* Nonblocking JavaScript

* Error-first callback

* The continuation-passing style

* Handling asynchronous functions in the ES7 way

* Parallel tasks and task series with the Async.js library

* Event handling optimization

Nonblocking JavaScript

First of all, let's look at what really happens when we do things asynchronously. Whenever we invoke a function in JavaScript, it creates a new stack frame (execution object). Every inner call gets into this frame. Here the frames are pushed and popped from the top of the call stack in the **LIFO (last in, first out)** manner. In other words, in the code, we call the foo function and then the bar function; however, during execution, foo calls the baz function. In this case, in the call stack, we have the following sequence: foo, baz, and only then bar. So bar is called after the stack frame of foo is empty. If any of the functions perform a CPU-intensive task, all the successive calls wait for it to finish. However, JavaScript engines have **Event Queues** (or task queues).

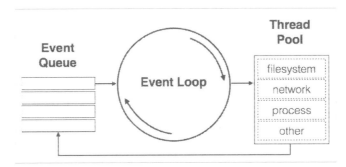

If we subscribe a function to a DOM event or pass a callback to a timer (setTimeout or setInterval) or through any Web I/O APIs (XHR, IndexedDB, and FileSystem), it ends up in a corresponding queue. Then, the browser's event loop decides when and which callback to push in the callback stack. Here is an example:

```
function foo(){
  console.log( "Calling Foo" );
}
function bar(){
  console.log( "Calling Bar" );
}
setTimeout(foo, 0 );
bar();
```

Using setTimeout(foo, 0), we state that foo shall be called immediately, and then we call bar. However, foo lands in a queue and the event loop puts it deeper in the call stack:

```
Calling Bar
Calling Foo
```

This also means that if the `foo` callback performs a CPU-intensive task, it doesn't block the main execution flow. Similarly, an asynchronously-made XHR/Fetch request doesn't lock up the interaction while waiting for the server's response:

```
function bar(){
  console.log( "Bar complete" );
}
fetch( "http://www.telize.com/jsonip" ).then(function( response ) {
  console.log( "Fetch complete" );
});
bar();


// Console:
// Bar complete
// Fetch complete
```

How does this apply to real-world applications? Here is a common flow:

```
"use strict";
// This statement loads imaginary AMD modules
// You can find details about AMD standard in
// "Chapter 2: Modular programming with JavaScript"
require([ "news", "Session", "User", "Ui" ], function ( News, Session,
User, Ui ) {
  var session = new Session(),
      news = new News(),
      ui = new Ui({ el: document.querySelector( "[data-bind=ui]" ) });
  // load news
 news.load( ui.update );
 //  authorize user
 session.authorize(function( token ){
   var user = new User( token );
   // load user data
   user.load(function(){
     ui.update();
     // load user profile picture
     user.loadProfilePicture( ui.update );
     // load user notifications
     user.loadNotifications( ui.update );
   });
 });
});
```

The loading of JavaScript dependencies is queued, so the browser can render and deliver the UI to the user without waiting for that. As soon as the scripts are fully loaded, the application pushes two new tasks to the queue: *load news* and *authorize user*. Again, none of them blocks the main thread. Only when any of these requests complete and the main thread gets involved, it enhances the UI according to the newly received data. As soon as a user is authorized and the session token is retrieved, we can load user data. After the task is completed, we queue new ones.

As you can see, asynchronous code is harder to read compared to synchronous one. The execution sequences can be quite complex. Besides, we have to take extra care for error control. When going for synchronous code, we can wrap a block of the program with `try`/`catch` and intercept any errors thrown during execution:

```
function foo(){
  throw new Error( "Foo throws an error" );
}
try {
  foo();
} catch( err ) {
  console.log( "The error is caught" );
}
```

However, if the call is queued, it slips out of the `try`/`catch` scope:

```
function foo(){
  throw new Error( "Foo throws an error" );
}
try {
  setTimeout(foo, 0 );
} catch( err ) {
  console.log( "The error is caught" );
}
```

Yeah, asynchronous programming has its quirks. To get a grip on this, we will examine the existing practices of writing asynchronous code.

So to make the code asynchronous, we queue a task and subscribe for an event that is fired when the task is complete. Actually, we go for *Event-Driven Programming*, and in particular, we apply a *PubSub* pattern. For example, the `EventTarget` interface, which we touched upon in *Chapter 3*, *DOM Scripting and AJAX*, in a nutshell, is about subscribing listeners to events on DOM elements and firing these events either from UI or programmatically:

```
var el = document.createElement( "div" );
    event = new CustomEvent( "foo", { detail: "foo data" });
el.addEventListener( "foo", function( e ){
```

```
  console.log( "Foo event captured: ", e.detail );
}, false );

el.dispatchEvent( event );

// Foo event captured: foo data
```

Behind the DOM, we use a similar principle, but implementations may differ. Probably the most popular interface is based on two main methods, `obj.on` (to subscribe a handler) and `obj.trigger` (to fire an event):

```
obj.on( "foo", function( data ){
  console.log( "Foo event captured: ", data );
});
obj.trigger( "foo", "foo data" );
```

This is how PubSub is implemented in abstraction frameworks, for example, Backbone. jQuery uses this interface on DOM events also. The interface gained its momentum through simplicity, but it doesn't really help with spaghetti code and doesn't cover error handling.

Error-first Callback

The pattern used across all the asynchronous methods in Node.js is called **Error-first Callback**. Here is an example:

```
fs.readFile( "foo.txt", function ( err, data ) {
  if ( err ) {
    console.error( err );
  }
  console.log( data );
});
```

Any asynchronous method expects one of the arguments to be a callback. The full callback argument list depends on the caller method, but the first argument is always an error object or null. When we go for the asynchronous method, an exception thrown during function execution cannot be detected in a `try`/`catch` statement. The event happens after the JavaScript engine leaves the `try` block. In the preceding example, if any exception is thrown during the reading of the file, it lands on the callback function as the first and mandatory parameter. Regardless of its widespread use, this approach has its flaws. While writing real code with deep callback sequences, it is easy to run into a so-called **Callback Hell** (`http://callbackhell.com/`). The code becomes pretty hard to follow.

Continuation-passing style

We often need a chain of asynchronous calls, that is, a sequence of tasks where one task is started after another is completed. We are interested in an eventual result of asynchronous calls chain. In this case, we can benefit from **Continuation-passing style (CPS)**. JavaScript has already a built-in `Promise` object. We use it to create a new `Promise` object. We put our asynchronous task in the `Promise` callback and invoke the `resolve` function of the argument list to notify the `Promise` callback that the task is resolved:

```javascript
"use strict";
    /**
     * Increment a given value
     * @param {Number} val
     * @returns {Promise}
     */
var foo = function( val ) {
    /**
     * Return a promise.
     * @param {Function} resolve
     */
    return new Promise(function( resolve ) {
      setTimeout(function(){
        resolve( val + 1 );
      }, 0 );
    });
    };

foo( 1 ).then(function( val ){
  console.log( "Result: ", val );
});

// Result: 5
```

In the preceding example, we called `foo`, that returns `Promise`. Using this method, we set a handler that invokes when `Promise` is fulfilled.

What about error control? When creating `Promise`, we can use the function given in the second argument (`reject`) to report a failure:

```javascript
"use strict";
/**
 * Make GET request
 * @param {String} url
 * @returns {Promise}
```

```
   */
function ajaxGet( url ) {
  return new Promise(function( resolve, reject ) {
    var req = new XMLHttpRequest();
    req.open( "GET", url );
    req.onload = function() {
      // If response status isn't 200 something went wrong
      if ( req.status !== 200 ) {
        // Early exit
        return reject( new Error( req.statusText ) );
      }
      // Everything is ok, we can resolve the promise
      return resolve( JSON.parse( req.responseText ) );
    };
    // On network errors
    req.onerror = function() {
      reject( new Error( "Network Error" ) );
    };
    // Make the request
    req.send();
  });
};

ajaxGet("http://www.telize.com/jsonip").then(function( data ){
  console.log( "Your IP is ", data.ip );
}).catch(function( err ){
  console.error( err );
});
// Your IP is 127.0.0.1
```

The most exciting part about `Promises` is that they can be chained. We can pipe the callbacks to queue asynchronous tasks or transform values:

```
"use strict";
  /**
   * Increment a given value
   * @param {Number} val
   * @returns {Promise}
   */
var foo = function( val ) {
    /**
     * Return a promise.
     * @param {Function} resolve
     * @param {Function} reject
     */
```

```
            return new Promise(function( resolve, reject ) {
                if ( !val ) {
                    return reject( new RangeError( "Value must be greater than
zero" ) );
                }
                setTimeout(function(){
                    resolve( val + 1 );
                }, 0 );
            });
        };

    foo( 1 ).then(function( val ){
        // chaining async call
        return foo( val );
    }).then(function( val ){
        // transforming output
        return val + 2;
    }).then(function( val ){
        console.log( "Result: ", val );
    }).catch(function( err ){
        console.error( "Error caught: ", err.message );
    });

    // Result: 5
```

Note that if we pass 0 to the foo function, the entry condition throws an exception and we will end up in a callback of the catch method. If an exception is thrown in one of the callbacks, it appears in the catch callback as well.

A Promise chain is resolved in a manner similar to that of a waterfall model—the tasks are invoked one after another. We can also cause Promise to resolve after several parallel processing tasks are completed:

```
    "use strict";
        /**
         * Increment a given value
         * @param {Number} val
         * @returns {Promise}
         */
    var foo = function( val ) {
            return new Promise(function( resolve ) {
                setTimeout(function(){
                    resolve( val + 1 );
                }, 100 );
            });
```

```
  },
  /**
   * Increment a given value
   * @param {Number} val
   * @returns {Promise}
   */
  bar = function( val ) {
    return new Promise(function( resolve ) {
      setTimeout(function(){
        resolve( val + 2 );
      }, 200 );
    });
  };

Promise.all([ foo( 1 ), bar( 2 ) ]).then(function( arr ){
  console.log( arr );
});
// [2, 4]
```

The `Promise.all` static method is not yet supported in all the latest browsers, but you can get this via a polyfill at `https://github.com/jakearchibald/es6-promise`.

Another probability is to cause `Promise` to resolve or reject whenever any of the concurrently running tasks are completed:

```
Promise.race([ foo( 1 ), bar( 2 ) ]).then(function( arr ){
  console.log( arr );
});
// 2
```

Handling asynchronous functions in the ES7 way

We already have the Promise API in JavaScript. The upcoming technology is Async/ Await API and is presented in a proposal (`https://tc39.github.io/ecmascript-asyncawait/`) for EcmaScript 7th edition. This describes how we can declare asynchronous functions that can halt without blocking anything and wait for the result of `Promise`:

```
"use strict";

// Fetch a random joke
function fetchQuote() {
  return fetch( "http://api.icndb.com/jokes/random" )
```

```
    .then(function( resp ){
      return resp.json();
    }).then(function( data ){
      return data.value.joke;
    });
}
// Report either a fetched joke or error
async function sayJoke()
{
  try {
    let result = await fetchQuote();
    console.log( "Joke:", result );
  } catch( err ) {
    console.error( err );
  }
}
sayJoke();
```

At the moment, the API isn't supported in any browser; however, you can run it using the Babel.js transpiler on runtime. You can also fiddle with this example online at http://codepen.io/dsheiko/pen/gaeqRO.

This new syntax allows us to write a code that runs asynchronously while appearing to be synchronous. Thus, we can use common constructions such as try/catch for asynchronous calls, which makes the code much more readable and easier to maintain.

Parallel tasks and task series with the Async.js library

Another approach to deal with asynchronous calls is a library called **Async.js** (https://github.com/caolan/async). When using this library, we can explicitly specify how we want the batch of tasks to be resolved—as a waterfall (chain) or in parallel.

In the first case, we can supply an array of callbacks to async.waterfall, assuming when one is completed, the next one is invoked. We can also pass the resolved value from one callback to another and receive the aggregate value or the thrown exception in a method's on-done callback:

```
/**
 * Concat given arguments
 * @returns {String}
```

```
 */
function concat(){
  var args = [].slice.call( arguments );
  return args.join( "," );
}


async.waterfall([
    function( cb ){
      setTimeout( function(){
        cb( null, concat( "foo" ) );
      }, 10 );
    },
    function( arg1, cb ){
      setTimeout( function(){
        cb( null, concat( arg1, "bar" ) );
      }, 0 );
    },
    function( arg1, cb ){
      setTimeout( function(){
        cb( null, concat( arg1, "baz" ) );
      }, 20 );
    }
], function( err, results ){
    if ( err ) {
      return console.error( err );
    }
    console.log( "All done:", results );
});


// All done: foo,bar,baz
```

Similarly, we pass an array of callbacks to `async.parallel`. This time, all of them run in parallel, but when all are resolved, we receive the results or the thrown exception in the method's `on-done` callback:

```
async.parallel([
    function( cb ){
      setTimeout( function(){
        console.log( "foo is complete" );
        cb( null, "foo" );
      }, 10 );
    },
    function( cb ){
      setTimeout( function(){
```

```
              console.log( "bar is complete" );
              cb( null, "bar" );
            }, 0 );
        },
        function( cb ){
          setTimeout( function(){
            console.log( "baz is complete" );
            cb( null, "baz" );
          }, 20 );
        }
], function( err, results ){
    if ( err ) {
      return console.error( err );
    }
    console.log( "All done:", results );
});

// bar is complete
// foo is complete
// baz is complete
// All done: [ 'foo', 'bar', 'baz' ]
```

Surely, we can combine the flows. Besides, the library provides iteration methods, such as `map`, `filter`, and `each`, that applies to the array of asynchronous tasks.

Async.js was the first project of this kind. Today, there are many libraries inspired by this. If you want a lightweight and robust solution similar to Async.js, I would recommend that you check Contra (`https://github.com/bevacqua/contra`).

Event handling optimization

It must have happened to you while writing a form inline validator that you run into a problem. As you type it, the `user-agent` keeps sending validation requests to the server. This way you might quickly pollute the network with spawning XHRs. Another sort of problem that you may be familiar with, is that some UI events (`touchmove`, `mousemove`, `scroll`, and `resize`) are fired intensively and subscribed handlers may overload the main thread. These problems can be solved using one of two approaches known as *debouncing* and *throttling*. Both functions are available in third-party libraries such as Underscore and Lodash (`_.debounce` and `_.throttle`). However, they can be implemented with a little o code and one doesn't need to depend on extra libraries for this functionality.

Debouncing

By debouncing, we ensure that a handler function is called once for a repeatedly emitted event:

```
/**
 * Invoke a given callback only after this function stops being
called `wait` milliseconds
 * usage:
 * debounce( cb, 500 )( ..arg );
 *
 * @param {Function} cb
 * @param {Number} wait
 * @param {Object} thisArg
 */
function debounce ( cb, wait, thisArg ) {
  /**
   * @type {number}
   */
  var timer = null;
  return function() {
    var context = thisArg || this,
        args = arguments;
    window.clearTimeout( timer );
    timer = window.setTimeout(function(){
      timer = null;
      cb.apply( context, args );
    }, wait );
  };
}
```

Let's say we want a widget to lazy load only when it comes into view, which in our case requires a user to scroll the page at least by 200 pixels downwards:

```
var TOP_OFFSET = 200;
// Lazy-loading
window.addEventListener( "scroll", debounce(function(){
  var scroll = window.scrollY || window.pageYOffset || document.
documentElement.scrollTop;
  if ( scroll >= TOP_OFFSET ){
    console.log( "Load the deferred widget (if not yet loaded)" );
  }
}, 20 ));
```

If we simply subscribe a listener to the scroll event, it will be called quite a number of times between the time interval when the user starts and stops scrolling. Thanks to the debounce proxy, the handler that checks whether it's the time to load the widget or not is called only once, when the user stops scrolling.

Throttling

By throttling, we set how often the handler is allowed to be called while the event is fired:

```
/**
 * Invoke a given callback every `wait` ms until this function stops
being called
 * usage:
 * throttle( cb, 500 )( ..arg );
 *
 * @param {Function} cb
 * @param {Number} wait
 * @param {Object} thisArg
 */
function throttle( cb, wait, thisArg ) {
  var prevTime,
      timer;
  return function(){
    var context = thisArg || this,
        now = +new Date(),
        args = arguments;

    if ( !prevTime || now >= prevTime + wait ) {
      prevTime = now;
      return cb.apply( context, args );
    }
    // hold on to it
    clearTimeout( timer );
    timer = setTimeout(function(){
      prevTime = now;
      cb.apply( context, args );
    }, wait );
  };
}
```

So if we subscribe a handler to the `mousemove` event on a container via throttle, the `handler` function once a time (second here) until the mouse cursors leaves the container boundaries:

```
document.body.addEventListener( "mousemove", throttle(function( e ){
  console.log( "The cursor is within the element at ", e.pageX, ",",
e.pageY );
}, 1000 ), false );

// The cursor is within the element at 946 , 715
// The cursor is within the element at 467 , 78
```

Writing callbacks that don't impact latency-critical events

Some of the tasks that we have do not belong to a core functionality and may run in the background. For example, we want to dispatch analytics data while scrolling. We do this without debouncing or throttling that would overload the UI thread and would likely make the app unresponsive. Debouncing isn't relevant here and throttling won't give precise data. However, we can use the `requestIdleCallback` native method (`https://w3c.github.io/requestidlecallback/`) to schedule the task at the time when `user-agent` is idle.

Summary

One of our most prioritized goals is to reduce user-response time, that is, the application architecture must ensure the user flow is never blocked. This can be achieved by queuing any long-running tasks for asynchronous invocation. However, if you have a number of asynchronous calls among which some are intended to run in parallel and some sequentially, without taking special care, it's easy to run into a so-called Callback Hell. A proper use of such approaches as *Continuation-passing style* (*Promise API*), the Async/Await API, or an external library such as Async.js may significantly improve your asynchronous code. We also have to remember that some events such as `scroll/touch/mousemove`, while being intensively fired, may cause unnecessary CPU load by calling subscribed listeners frequently. We can avoid these problems using debouncing and throttling techniques.

By learning the basis of asynchronous programming, we can write nonblocking applications. In *Chapter 6, A Large-Scale JavaScript Application Architecture*, we will talk about how to make our applications scalable and improve the maintainability in general.

6

A Large-Scale JavaScript Application Architecture

Any experienced programmer works hard to make the code reusable and maintainable. Here we are guided by the principles of object-oriented programming, such as encapsulation, abstraction, inheritance, composition, and polymorphism. In addition to these fundamentals, we follow the *five basic principles* of object-oriented programming and design defined by Robert C. Martin and known under the acronym **SOLID** (`https://en.wikipedia.org/wiki/SOLID_(object-oriented_design)`). When during code review we run into a violation of any of these principles, it's considered as a code smell and results in refactoring. At the core of the tasks that we solve every day in development, often lie the common problems that we meet again and again. In this chapter, we will cover the most common universal architectural solutions and concepts in JavaScript development:

- Design patterns in JavaScript
- Understanding concern separation in JavaScript using JavaScript MV* Frameworks

Design patterns in JavaScript

Abstract bulletproof solutions have been known for long and are usually referred to as **Design Patterns**. The original 23 Design Patterns in programming were first collected in *Design Patterns: Elements of Reusable Object-Oriented Software*, an influential book published in 1995 by *Erich Gamma*, *Richard Helm*, *Ralph Johnson*, and *John Vlissides* (*GoF*). These patterns are language-agnostic. Nonetheless, *Addy Osmani* in his online book *Learning JavaScript Design Patterns* (`http://addyosmani.com/resources/essentialjsdesignpatterns/book/`) shows how some of the GoF's patterns can be implemented particularly in JavaScript.

Here we won't repeat his work; instead we'll examine how we can combine the patterns. One of the common problems in JavaScript development is communication between dynamically created objects. For instance, we have an object and need to call a method (baz) of object bar from foo. However, we cannot know if bar is already available. GoF's pattern mediator encourages us to dedicate an object that is used to proxy communications between other objects. Thus, we promote loose coupling by keeping objects from direct interaction. In our case, despite calling bar.baz, we inform the mediator about our intent. The mediator will do the call when bar is available:

```
"use strict";

class EventEmitter {
  /** Initialize */
  constructor() {
    /**
     * @access private
     * @type {EventHandler[]}
     */
    this.handlers = [];
  }
  /**
   * Subscribe a cb handler for a given event in the object scope
   * @param {String} ev
   * @param {Function} cb
   * @param {Object} [context]
   * @returns {EventEmitter}
   */
  on( ev, cb, context ){
    this.handlers.push({
      event: ev,
      callback: cb,
      context: context
    });
    return this;
  }
  /**
   * Emit a given event in the object
   * @param {String} ev
   * @param {...*} [arg]
   * @returns {EventEmitter}
   */
  trigger( ev, ...args ) {
    this.handlers.forEach(function( evObj ){
```

```
    if ( evObj.event !== ev || !evObj.callback.apply ) {
      return;
    }
    evObj.callback.apply( evObj.context || this, args );
  }, this );
  return this;
  }
}


window.mediator = new EventEmitter();
```

Here, we used the ES6 syntax, which serves just perfectly to describe a code design. With ES6, the intend can be shown to be concise and plain, while in the JavaScript edition ES5 and older we need additional lines of code to achieve the same result.

In the preceding example, we created a mediator object by instantiating the `EventEmitter` class. `EventEmitter` implements a messaging pattern known as PubSub. This pattern describes a message exchange where one object sends an event addressed to another object and the second object calls the handlers, if any, which subscribed for the event. In other words, if we subscribe a handler function of the `foo` object for the `myevent` mediator event (`mediator.on`), we can then invoke the handler of `foo` from any other object by publishing the `myevent` event on the mediator (`mediator.trigger`). Let's look at an example. Our imaginary application is localized. It starts with a login screen. When users signs in, the screen jumps to the dashboard with the news. User may change the language on any of the screens. However, in the first stage, the news view object isn't yet even created, while in the second stage, the login view object is already destroyed. However, if we use the mediator, we can trigger the `translate` event and all the available subscribers will receive the message:

```
class News {
  /** Initialize */
  constructor(){
    mediator.on( "translate", this.update, this );
  }
  /** @param {String} lang */
  update( lang ){
    // fetch news from remote host for a given lang
    console.log( "News loaded for", lang );
  }
}

class Language {
  /** @param {String} lang */
  change( lang ) {
```

```
      mediator.trigger( "translate", lang );
  }
}

let language = new Language();
new News()
language.change( "de" );
```

Whenever a user changes the language (`language.change`), the corresponding event is broadcasted through the mediator. When the news instance is available, it calls the `update` method that receives an event payload. In a real application, this instance would load news for the given language and update the view.

So what did we achieve? When using a mediator and an event-driven approach (PubSub), our objects/modules are loosely coupled and therefore, the overall architecture better accepts requirement changes. Besides, we gain more flexibility in unit testing.

At the time this book was written, no browser provided native support for the ES6 class statement. However, you can run the given code using Babel.js run-time (`https://babeljs.io/docs/usage/browser/`) or transpiring.

When the application grows and we are getting too many events that are circulating, it makes sense to encapsulate event handling into a separate message hub object. Here comes to mind the `Facade` pattern, which defines a unified high-level interface for other interfaces:

```
class Facade {
  constructor(){
    mediator.on( "show-dashboard", function(){
      this.dashboard.show()
      this.userPanel.remove();
    }, this )
    .on( "show-userpanel", function(a){
      this.dashboard.hide()
      this.userPanel = new UserPanel( this.user );
    }, this )
    .on( "authorized", function( user ){
      this.user = user;
      this.topBar = new TopBar( user.name );
      this.dashboard = new Dashboard( user.lang );
      this.mainMenu = new MainMenu( user.lang );
    }, this )
    .on( "logout", function(){
      this.userPanel.remove();
```

```
      this.topBar.remove();
      this.dashboard.remove();
      this.mainMenu.remove();
      this.login = new Login();
    }, this );
  }
}
```

After initializing the `Facade` class, we can trigger a complex flow where multiple modules are involved by simply firing an event on the mediator. This way we encapsulate behavioral logic into a dedicated object; this makes the code more readable and the whole system easier to maintain.

Understanding concern separation in JavaScript

While writing JavaScript (especially client-side), one of the major challenges is to avoid *spaghetti code*, where the same module renders the user view, handles user interactions, and does the business logic. Such a module may quickly grow into a monster of a source file, where a developer rather gets lost than spots and resolves a problem.

The MVC Programming paradigm known as **Model View Controller** (**MVC**) splits the application functionality into separate layers such as presentation, data, and user input. MVC in a nutshell implies that a user interacts with the view land in a controller module that manipulates a model, which updates the view. In JavaScript, the controller is usually an observer that listens to UI events. A user clicks a button, the event is fired, and the controller addresses the corresponding model. For example, the controller requests the model to send submitted data to the server. The view is notified about the model state change and reacts accordingly, let's say it displays a message, **Data saved**. Collaboration of components in MVC pattern is shown in the following image:

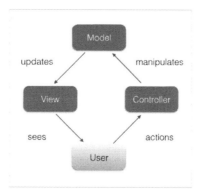

As you see, we can keep all the user input handlers encapsulated in a single module (here the **Controller**), we can abstract the data layer following Domain-Driven design practices into a model module. Eventually, we have a view module responsible for updating the UI. So, the model has no knowledge about the component's presentation (HTML, CSS) and knows nothing about DOM events—that's just pure data and operations on it. The controller knows only the events from the view and the view API. And finally, the view knows nothing about the model and controller, but exposes its API and sends events. Thus, we have an efficient architecture that is easy to maintain and test.

However, in the case of a JavaScript-built UI, it's not that easy to draw a line between the view logic and the controller one. Here we get handy MVC derivatives: **MVP** and **MVVM.MVP**.

The **P** in **MVP** stands for **Presenter** that serves user requests. The presenter listens to the view events, retrieves data, manipulates it, and updates the presentation using the view API. The **Presenter** can interact with models to persist data. As you can see in the following diagram, the **Presenter** acts like a manager that receives a request, processes it using available resources, and directs the view to change. Following image shows collaboration of components in MVP pattern:

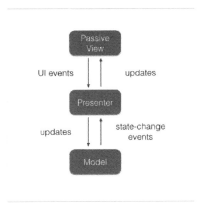

MVP provides better testability and concern separation compared to MVC. You can find an example of a TODO application implementing MVP at http://codepen.io/dsheiko/pen/WQymbG.

MVVM

A passive view of MVP is mostly about data bindings and proxying of UI events. In fact, that's something we can abstract. The view in **Model View ViewModel (MVVM)** approach may not require any JavaScript at all. Usually, the view is HTML-extended with directives known by ViewModel. The model represents domain-specific data and exposes concomitant methods such as validation. The ViewModel is a middleman between view and model. It converts the data objects from the model for the view. For instance, when a model property contains a raw datetime, the ViewModel converts it into the form expected in the view like `1 January 2016, 00:01`. Following image shows collaboration of components in MVVM pattern:

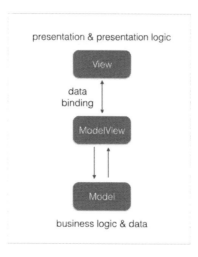

The MVVM pattern has the advantage of both imperative and declarative programming. It may drastically reduce the development time by abstracting most of the generic view logic in a common binder module. The pattern gains momentum with popular JavaScript frameworks such as Knockout, Angular, and Meteor. You can find an example of an RSS reader application based on MVVM pattern at `https://msdn.microsoft.com/en-us/magazine/hh297451.aspx`.

Using JavaScript MV* frameworks

When starting a new scalable web application, you have to decide whether to go with a framework or not. It's hard now to find any large projects that are not built on the top of a framework. Yet there are drawbacks in using frameworks; just take a look at **Zero Framework Manifesto** (`http://bitworking.org/news/2014/05/zero_ framework_manifesto`). However, if you decide in favor of frameworks, then you are in a quandary about which one to pick. This is indeed not an easy task. JavaScript frameworks today are quite numerous; just take a look at the variety available at TodoMVC (`http://todomvc.com`). It's hardly feasible to review all of them, but we can briefly examine a few of the most popular frameworks. According to recent surveys (for example, `http://ashleynolan.co.uk/blog/frontend-tooling- survey-2015-results`), among the most trendy are Angular, React, and Backbone. All three give quite dissimilar development paradigms. So they are fitting to make an overall picture of JavaScript frameworks in general.

Backbone

Backbone (`http://backbonejs.org`) is very lightweight and easy to start with. This is the only popular framework where you can grasp the entire codebase in a considerably short time (`http://backbonejs.org/docs/backbone.html`). Inherently, Backbone gives you a consistent abstraction and nothing besides this. By and large, we encapsulate all the UI-related logic into a subtype of `Backbone.View`. Any data required by the view, we put this into a derivative of `Backbone.Model` or `Backbone.Collection` (when it's a list of entries). Eventually, we route hash-based navigation requests by means of `Backbone.Route`.

Let's consider an example. Our imaginary application allows us to look up for a contact by a given email address. Since we want this to be user friendly, the application form is expected to validate as we type in it. For this, we need a little HTML:

```
<form data-bind="fooForm">
    <label for="email">Email:</label>
    <input id="email" name="email" required />
    <span class="error-msg" data-bind="errorMsg"></span>
    <button data-bind="submitBtn" type="submit">Submit</button>
</form>
```

Here we have an input control, a submit button, and a container for a possible error message. In order to manage this, we will use the following `Backbone.View`:

ContactSearchView.js

```javascript
"use strict";
/** @class {ContactSearchView}  */
var ContactSearchView = Backbone.View.extend(/** @lends
ContactSearchView.prototype */{
  events: {
    "submit": "onSubmit"
  },
  /** @constructs {ContactSearchView} */
  initialize: function() {
    this.$email = this.$el.find( "[name=email]" );
    this.$errorMsg = this.$el.find( "[data-bind=errorMsg]" );
    this.$submitBtn = this.$el.find( "[data-bind=submitBtn]" );
    this.bindUi();
  },
  /** Bind handlers */
  bindUi: function(){
    this.$email.on( "input", this.onChange.bind( this ) );
    this.model.on( "invalid", this.onInvalid.bind( this ) );
    this.model.on( "change", this.onValid.bind( this ) );
  },
  /** Handle input onchange event */
  onChange: function(){
    this.model.set({
      email: this.$email.val(),
      // Hack to force model running validation on repeating payloads
      "model:state": ( 1 + Math.random() ) * 0x10000
    }, { validate: true });
  },
  /** Handle model in invalid state */
  onInvalid: function(){
    var error = arguments[ 1 ];
    this.$errorMsg.text( error );
    this.$submitBtn.prop( "disabled", "disabled" );
  },
  /** Handle model in valid state */
  onValid: function(){
    this.$errorMsg.empty();
    this.$submitBtn.removeProp( "disabled" );
  },
  /** Handle form submit */
  onSubmit: function( e ){
```

```
      e.preventDefault();
      alert( "Looking up for " + this.model.get( "email") );
   }
});
```

In the constructor (the `initialize` method), we bind the acting nodes of the HTML to the properties of the view and subscribe handlers to UI and the model events. Then, we register listener methods on the `submit` form and the `input` form. The second handler is invoked as we type, and it updates the model. The model runs a validation, and according to the results, it responds with a `invalid` or `change` model event. In the case of the `invalid` event, the view shows up the error message, otherwise it's hidden.

Now we can add the model, as shown here:

ContactSearchModel.js

```
  "use strict";
/** @class {ContactSearchModel}  */
var ContactSearchModel = Backbone.Model.extend(/** @lends
ContactSearchModel.prototype */{
  /** @type {Object} */
  defaults: {
    email: ""
  },
  /**
   * Validate email
   * @param {String} email
   */
  isEmailValid: function( email ) {
    var pattern = /^[a-zA-Z0-9\!\#\$\%\&\'\*\+\-\/\=\?\^\_\`\
{\|\}\~\.]+@[a-zA-Z0-9.\-]+\.[a-zA-Z]{2,4}$/g;
    return email.length && pattern.test( email );
  },
  /**
   * Validate model
   * @param {Map} attrs
   */
  validate: function( attrs ) {
    if ( !attrs.email ) {
      return "Email is required.";
    }
    if ( !this.isEmailValid( attrs.email ) ) {
      return "Invalid email address.";
    }
  }
});
```

This model defines domain data in the `defaults` property and provides the `validate` method that is called automatically when we set or save the model.

Now we can combine all together and initialize the view:

```
<!DOCTYPE html>
<html>
  <script type="text/javascript" src="//ajax.googleapis.com/ajax/libs/
jquery/1.11.3/jquery.min.js"></script>
  <script type="text/javascript" src="//cdnjs.cloudflare.com/ajax/
libs/underscore.js/1.5.2/underscore-min.js"></script>
  <script type="text/javascript" src="//cdnjs.cloudflare.com/ajax/
libs/backbone.js/1.0.0/backbone-min.js"></script>
  <script type="text/javascript" src="ContactSearchView.js"></script>
  <script type="text/javascript" src="ContactSearchModel.js"></script>
  <style>
    fieldset { border: 0; }
    .error-msg{ color: red; }
  </style>
  <body>
   <form data-bind="fooForm">
    <fieldset>
      <label for="email">Email:</label>
      <input id="email" name="email" required />
      <span class="error-msg" data-bind="errorMsg"></span>
    </fieldset>
    <fieldset>
      <button data-bind="submitBtn" type="submit">Submit</button>
    </fieldset>
   </form>
<script>

// Render foo view
 new ContactSearchView({
   el: $( "[data-bind=fooForm]" ),
   model: new ContactSearchModel
 });

</script>
  </body>
</html>
```

Backbone itself is surprisingly small in size (6.5 Kg zipped), but with the jQuery and Underscore dependencies, this makes quite a bundle. Both dependencies were vital in the past, but now that's under the question — do we need them at all? So, it makes sense to check the **Exoskeleton** (http://exosjs.com/) project, which is an optimized version of Backbone that works perfectly without the dependencies.

Angular

Angular (http://Angular.org) now seems to be the most popular JavaScript framework in the world. It is supported by Google and is considered as a framework that solves most routine tasks for you. In particular, Angular has a feature called two-way binding, meaning that UI changes propagate to the bound model and, vice versa, and model changes (for example, by XHR) update the UI.

In AngularJS, we define behavior straight in HTML with directives. Directives are custom elements and attributes that assume UI logic similar to web components. Actually, you can create functional widgets in AngularJS without writing a single line of JavaScript code. Models in AngularJS are simple data containers and unlike Backbone, have no connection to external sources. When we need to read or write data, we use services. When any data is sent to View, we can use filters to format the output. The framework leverages dependency injection (DI) pattern allowing to inject core components into each other as dependencies. That makes the modules easier to meet requirement changes and unit-test. Let's see this in practice:

```html
<!DOCTYPE html>
<html>
  <script src="http://ajax.googleapis.com/ajax/libs/Angular/1.3.14/
angular.min.js"></script>
  <style>
    fieldset { border: 0; }
    .error-msg{ color: red; }
  </style>
  <body>
    <form ng-app="contactSearch" name="csForm" ng-submit="submit()" ng-
controller="csController">
      <fieldset>
        <label for="email">Email:</label>
        <input id="email" name="email" ng-model="email" required
            ng-pattern="/^[a-zA-Z0-9\!\#\$\%\&\'\*\+\-\/\=\?\^\_\`\
{\|\}\~\.]+@[a-zA-Z0-9.\-]+\.[a-zA-Z]{2,4}$/"  />
        <span class="error-msg" ng-show="csForm.email.$dirty && csForm.
email.$invalid">
          <span ng-show="csForm.email.$error.required">Email is
required.</span>
```

```
            <span ng-show="csForm.email.$error.pattern">Invalid email
address.</span>
        </span>
    </fieldset>
    <fieldset>
        <button type="submit" ng-disabled="csForm.email.$dirty &&
csForm.email.$invalid">Submit</button>
    </fieldset>
  </form>
<script>
  "use strict";
  angular.module( "contactSearch", [] ).controller( "csController", [
"$scope", function ( $scope ){
    $scope.email = "";
    $scope.submit = function() {
      alert( "Looking up for " + $scope.email );
    };
  }]);
</script>
  </body>
</html>
```

In this example, we declared an input field and bound it to a model email
(ng-model directive). Form validation works in the same way as in HTML5 forms: if
we declare an input type email and it gets validated accordingly. Here we go with a
default text type and use the ng-pattern (similar to HTML5's pattern) attribute to
set the same validation rules for email as in the Backbone case. Further, we rely on
the ng-show directive to display error messages block when the input state is empty
(csForm.email.$dirty) or invalid (csForm.email.$invalid). In this case, the
submit button, on the contrary, is hidden. Using the ng-controller and ng-submit
directives, we bind the csController controller and the on-submit handler to the
form. In the body of csController (JavaScript), $scope.submit expects a handler
function for the form submit event.

As you can see with Angular, it takes much less code in total to implement the same
task. However, one should accept that keeping application logic in HTML makes it
really hard to read the code.

Furthermore, Angular subscribes many watchers per directive (intended handlers,
automatic dirty checking, and so on) and makes it slow and resource-expensive on
the pages with numerous interactive elements. If you want to tune your application
performance, you rather learn Angular source code and it'll be a challenging task
with ~11.2K lines of code (version 1.4.6).

React

React (`https://facebook.github.io`) is a project of Facebook that isn't really a framework, but rather a library. The unique approach of React implies a component-based application. Inherently, React defines the Views of the components utilizing the so-called Virtual DOM, which makes UI rendering and updating surprisingly fast. With this focus on View, React comprises a template engine. Optionally, the React components can be written in a subset of JavaScript called JSX where you can put HTML templates within JavaScript. JSX can be parsed dynamically as in the following example, or it can be precompiled. Since React deals with Views only and makes no assumptions about other concerns, it makes sense to use this in conjunction with other frameworks. Thus, React can be plugged into a framework (for example, as directives in Angular or Views in Backbone).

While implementing the contact search application this time, we will use React to control the View of our example by splitting it into two components (`FormView` and `EmailView`). The first one defines the View for the search form:

```
    /** @class {FormView}  */
var FormView = React.createClass({
  /** Create an initial state with the model  */
  getInitialState: function () {
    return {
      email: new EmailModel()
    };
  },
  /**
   * Update state on input change event
   * @param {String} value - changed value of the input
   */
  onChange: function( value ){
    this.state.email.set( "email", value );
    this.forceUpdate();
  },
  /** Handle form submit */
  onSubmit: function( e ){
    e.preventDefault();
    alert( "Looking up for " + this.state.email.get( "email") );
  },
  /** Render form */
  render: function () {
    return <form onSubmit={this.onSubmit}>
      <fieldset>
      <label htmlFor="email">Email:</label>
```

```
      <EmailView model={this.state.email} onChange={this.onChange} />
      </fieldset>
      <fieldset>
        <button data-bind="submitBtn" type="submit">Submit</button>
      </fieldset>
    </form>;
  }
});
```

In the `render` method, we declared the View of the component using the JSX notation. This makes it much easier to manipulate the Virtual DOM. Similar to Angular, we can address the component scope directly in the HTML. Thus, we subscribe to the form submit event and to the input change event by referring to the corresponding handlers in the `onSubmit` and `onChange` attributes. Since React provides no built-in model, we reused `ContactSearchModel`, the model we created while exploring Backbone.

You might notice a `EmailView` custom tag in JSX. This is how we refer to our second component, which represents an email input control:

```
    /** @class {EmailView}  */
  var EmailView = React.createClass({
    /**
     * Delegate input on-changed event to the from view
     * @param {Event} e
     */
    onChanged: function( e ){
      this.props.onChange( e.target.value );
    },
    /** Render input */
    render: function () {
      var model = this.props.model;
      return <span>
        <input id="email" type="text" value={model.email}
  onChange={this.onChanged} />
        <span className="error-msg" data-bind="errorMsg">
  {model.isValid() ? "" : model.validationError}</span>
      </span>;
    }
  });
```

Here we bound the email input to the model and the error message container to the model state. We also passed the input `onChange` event to the parent component.

Well, now we can add the components in the HTML and render the form:

```html
<!DOCTYPE html>
<html>
<head>
  <script src="https://cdnjs.cloudflare.com/ajax/libs/react/0.13.3/
react.js"></script>
  <script src="https://cdnjs.cloudflare.com/ajax/libs/react/0.13.3/
JSXTransformer.js"></script>
  <script type="text/javascript" src="//cdnjs.cloudflare.com/ajax/
libs/underscore.js/1.5.2/underscore-min.js"></script>
  <script type="text/javascript" src="//cdnjs.cloudflare.com/ajax/
libs/backbone.js/1.0.0/backbone-min.js"></script>
  <script type="text/javascript" src="ContactSearchModel.js"></script>
  <style>
    fieldset { border: 0; }
    .error-msg{ color: red; }
  </style>
</head>
<body>
  <div data-bind="app"></div>
<script type="text/jsx">
  /** @jsx React.DOM */

// Please insert here both components
// FormView and EmailView

// render app
React.render(
  <FormView />,
  document.querySelector( "[data-bind=app]" )
);
</script>
</body>
</html>
```

We address the components in the templates such as web-components by the corresponding custom elements. Do not confuse yourself over the similarity, React components are abstracted from the browser, while web-components work similar to browser-native things. The core concept of React is that the Virtual DOM allows us to avoid unnecessary DOM reflow cycles that make the library preferable for high-performance applications. React is really good to render static pages on the server using Node.js. Thus, we can reuse application components between server and client sides.

Summary

Writing maintainable code is an art. Probably the best book that provides guidance on this is *Clean Code: A Handbook of Agile Software Craftsmanship* by *Robert C. Martin*. It's about naming functions, methods, classes, commenting, code formatting, and of course, about the correct use of OOP and SOLID. However, when reusing solutions described in this book, or in any of the Design Patterns series, we have to translate them into JavaScript, and it can be challenging due to the nature of the language. On a higher level, we have to split the code into layers such as presentation, business logic, data access, and persistence, where each bundle of code addresses the one concern and is loosely coupled with others. Here, we may choose an approach to go with. In the JavaScript world, it's usually a derivative of MVC (MVP or MVVM or other). Considering this, a decent programming design requires a lot of abstraction. Today, we can use numerous frameworks. They provide diverse programming paradigms.

7

JavaScript Beyond
the Browser

Originally, JavaScript was designed as a client-side scripting language, but today, it is used literally everywhere: in server scripting, mobile and desktop software programming, game development, DB querying, hardware control, and OS automation. When you have experience in client-side JavaScript, with a little additional knowledge, you can apply your skills in other programming areas as well. Here, we will learn how to write a command-line tool, web-server, desktop application, and mobile software using JavaScript.

In this chapter, we will be learning about the following:

- Leveling up the coding of a command-line program in JavaScript
- Building a web-server with JavaScript
- Writing a desktop HTML5 application
- Using PhoneGap to make a mobile native app

Levelling up the coding of a command-line program in JavaScript

You must have heard about Node.js. This is an open source cross-platform development environment that allows the creation of web-servers, networking, and other tools using JavaScript. Node.js extends classical JavaScript with a collection of specialized modules. These modules handle filesystem I/O, networking, OS-level operations, binary data, cryptography functions, data streams, and others (`https://nodejs.org/api/index.html`). Node.js uses an event-driven I/O model. Similar to JavaScript, it operates on single-thread performing non-blocking calls. So time consuming functions can run concurrently by invoking a callback when it completes.

To get the feel of Node.js, we start with an example that simply prints *Hello world*:

hello.js

```
console.log( "Hello world!" );
```

Now let's open the console (command-line interface: **CMD** in Windows, or **Terminal** in Linux and Mac OS), navigate to the example script location, and run the following:

```
node hello.js
```

Here we go, we get `Hello world!` in the output.

Following screenshot shows the Windows CMD

The Node.js modules follow the CommonJS specification in the same way that we examined in *Chapter 2, Modular Programming with JavaScript*:

foo.js

```
console.log( "Running foo.js" );
module.exports = "foo";
main.js
var foo = require( "./foo" );
console.log( "Running main.js" );
console.log( "Exported value:", foo );
```

As we run `main.js`, we are supposed to get the following output:

```
Running foo.js
Running main.js
Exported value: foo
```

The Node.js native modules such as `fs` (`https://nodejs.org/api/index.html`) don't require downloading. We may just refer to them in `require()`, and at the runtime, it will be known where to find them:

```
"use strict";
var fs = require( "fs" );
fs.readFile( __filename, "UTF-8", function( err, data ){
  if ( err ) {
    throw new Error( err );
  }
  console.log( "Source of ", __filename, ":\n", data );
});
```

Here we use the filesystem I/O (`fs`) module to read a file. The `__filename` property of a module scope contains the absolute path of the executing source file. Remember the *Error First Callback* approach that we examined in *Chapter 5, Asynchronous JavaScript* That is the main interface for asynchronous functions in Node.js.

Let's now try something more practical. We'll write a utility that recursively scans all the source files in a given directory to make sure every file has block comments with up-to-date copyrights. First of all, we need a module that can test whether a supplied block comment text contains the actual copyright line:

```
./Lib/BlockComment.js
  /**
   * Block comment entity
   * @class
   * @param {String} code
   */
var BlockComment = function( code ){
  return {
    /**
     * Check a block comment
     * @returns {Boolean}
     */
    isValid: function(){
      var lines = code.split( "\n" );
      return lines.some(function( line ){
          var date = new Date();
          return line.indexOf( "@copyright " + date.getFullYear() )
!== -1;
      });
    }
  };
};

module.exports = BlockComment;
```

Here, we have a constructor that creates an object representing `BlockComment`. The object has a method (`isValid`) to test its validity. So if we create an instance of `BlockComment` with a block comment text, we can validate this against our requirements:

```
var comment = new BlockComment( "/**\n* @copyright 2015 \n*/" );
comment.isValid() // true
```

Now, we will write a module capable of testing whether all the copyright lines in a given source code has the actual year:

```
./Lib/SourceFile.js
    /** @type {module:esprima} */
var esprima = require( "esprima" ),

/**
 * Source file entity
 * @class
 * @param {String} fileSrc
 * @param {module:Lib/BlockComment} BlockComment - dependency
injection
 */
SourceFile = function( fileSrc, BlockComment ){
  return {
    /**
     * Test if source file has valid copyright
     */
    isValid: function() {
      var blockComments = this.parse( fileSrc );
      return Boolean( blockComments.filter(function( comment ){
        return comment.isValid();
      }).length );
    },
    /**
     * Extract all the block comments as array of BlockComment
instances
     * @param {String} src
     * @returns {Array} - collection of BlockComment
     */
    parse: function( src ){
      return esprima.parse( src, {
        comment: true
      }).comments.filter(function( item ){
        return item.type === "Block";
      }).map(function( item ){
```

```
            return new BlockComment( item.value );
        });
    }

    };
};

module.exports = SourceFile;
```

In this example we introduced a `SourceFile` object that has two methods, `parse` and `isValid`. The private method, `parse`, extracts all the block comments from a given JavaScript source code and returns an array of the `BlockComment` objects. The `isValid` method checks whether all the received `BlockComment` objects meet our requirements. In these methods, to manipulate arrays, we use `Array.prototype.filter` and `Array.prototype.map` that we examined in *Chapter 1, Diving into JavaScript Core*.

But how can we reliably extract `blockComments` from a JavaScript source? The best way is to go with a bulletproof solution called the **esprima** parser (`http://esprima.org/`) that performs code static analysis and returns a full syntax tree including comments. However, esprima is a third-party package that is supposed to be downloaded and linked from the application. In general, a package may depend on other packages, which also have dependencies. It looks like that bringing the required dependencies together may be a hell of a work. Fortunately, Node.js is distributed with the NPM package manager. The tool can be used to install and manage in the NPM repository (`https://www.npmjs.com/`) third-party modules. NPM doesn't just download the requested modules, but also resolves the module dependencies, allowing a well-grained structure of reusable components in the scope of a project or in the global scope.

So, to make `esprima` available in our application, we simply request it from NPM using this command: `npm install esprima`.

By running this command in the console, we automatically get a new `node_modules` subdirectory with the `esprima` package in it. If the package requires any dependencies, they will be fetched and allocated in `node_modules`. As soon as the package is installed by NPM, Node.js can find it by its name. For example, `require( "esprima" )`. Now when we have the `SourceFile` object, we just need the main script that will read the files from a given directory and test them with `SourceFile`:

copyright-checker.js

```
        /** @type {module:cli-color} */
var clc = require( "cli-color" ),
    /** @type {module:fs-walk} */
    walk = require( "fs-walk" ),
    /** @type {module:path} */
```

```
        path = require( "path" ),
        /** @type {module:fs} */
        fs = require( "fs" ),
        /**
         * Source file entity
         * @type {module:Lib/SourceFile}
         */
        SourceFile = require( "./Lib/SourceFile" ),
        /** @type {module:Lib/BlockComment} */
        BlockComment = require( "./Lib/BlockComment" ),
        /**
         * Command-line first argument (if none given, go with ".")
         * @type {String}
         */
        dir = process.argv[ 2 ] || ".";

console.log( "Checking in " + clc.yellow( dir ) );

// Traverse directory tree recursively beginning from 'dir'
walk.files( dir, function( basedir, filename ) {
        /** @type {Function} */
    var next = arguments[ 3 ],
        /** @type {String} */
        fpath = path.join( basedir, filename ),
        /** @type {String} */
        fileSrc = fs.readFileSync( fpath, "UTF-8" ),
        /**
         * Get entity associated with the file located in fpath
         * @type {SourceFile}
         */
        file = new SourceFile( fileSrc, BlockComment );
    // ignore non-js files
    if ( !filename.match( /\.js$/i ) ) {
      return next();
    }
    if ( file.isValid() ) {
      console.log( fpath + ": " + clc.green( "valid" ) );
    } else {
      console.log( fpath + ": " + clc.red( "invalid" ) );
    }
    next();
}, function( err ) {
  err && console.log( err );
});
```

In this code, we relied on a third-party module, `cli-color`, to colorize the command-line output. We used the `fs-walk` module to recursively traverse through a directory. And the Node.js native module, path, allows us to resolve the absolute path by a given relative directory and filename, and the `fs` built-in module is used to read a file.

As we intend to run our application from the console, we can use command-line options to pass on a directory that we want to test:

```
node copyright-checker.js some-dir
```

We can extract script arguments from a built-in process (`process.argv`) object. For this command, `process.argv` will contain an array like this:

```
[ "node", "/AbsolutePath/copyright-checker.js", "some-dir" ]
```

So in the main script, now we can pass the third element of this array to `walk.files`. The function will traverse through the given directory and run the callback for every file found. In the callback function, if a filename looks like JavaScript, we read the content and test it using the `SourceFile` object.

Before we can run the main script, we need to ask NPM for third-party packages that we are going to use in the script:

```
npm install fs-walk cli-color
```

Now we are good to go. As we run `node copyright-checker.js fixtures`, we get a report on the validity of the JavaScript files located in fixtures.

Following screenshot shows the Mac OS X terminal:

Building a web server with JavaScript

We've just learnt how to write command-line scripts with Node.js. However, this run-time is mostly known as server-side JavaScript, meaning this is the software to run an HTTP-server. Actually, Node.js is especially great for this kind of job. If we launch a server application based on Node.js, it runs permanently, initialized only once. For instance, we may create a single DB connection object and reuse it whenever someone requests the application. Besides, it grants us all the flexibility and power of JavaScript including event-driven, non-blocking I/O.

So how can we make use of this? Thanks to the HTTP native module of Node.js, a simple web-server can be implemented as easy as this:

```
simple-server.js
"use strict";
    /** @type {module:http}  */
var http = require( "http" ),
    /** @type {HttpServer}  */
    server = http.createServer(function( request, response ) {
       response.writeHead( 200, {"Content-Type": "text/html"} );
       response.write( "<h1>Requested: " + request.url + "</h1>" );
       response.end();
    });

server.listen( 80 );
console.log( "Server is listening..." );
```

Here we created a server with a dispatcher callback to handle HTTP requests. Then, we make the server listen on port 80. Now run `node simple-server.js` from the console, and then hit `http://localhost` in a browser. We will see the following:

```
Requested: /
```

So we just need to route incoming requests, read the corresponding HTML files, and send them with the response to make a simple static web server. Or we can install the existing modules, `connect` and `serve-static`:

```
npm install connect serve-static
```

And implement the server using this:

```
"use strict";
    /** @type {module:connect}  */
var connect = require( "connect" ),
    /** @type {module:serve-static}  */
    serveStatic = require( "serve-static" );

connect().use( serveStatic( __dirname ) ).listen( 80 );
```

In practice, routing requests can be a challenging task, so we rather go with a framework. For example, Express.js (http://expressjs.com). Then, our routing may look like this:

```
"use strict";
    /** @type {module:express}  */
var express = require( "express" ),
    /** @type {module:http}  */
    http = require( "http" ),
    /** @type {Object}  */
    app = express();
// Send common HTTP header for every incoming request
app.all( "*", function( request, response, next ) {
  response.writeHead( 200, { "Content-Type": "text/plain" } );
  next();
});
// Say hello for the landing page
app.get( "/", function( request, response ) {
  response.end( "Welcome to the homepage!" );
});
// Show use if for requests like http://localhost/user/1
app.get( "/user/:id", function( request, response ) {
  response.end( "Requested ID: "  + req.params.id );
});
// Show `Page not found` for any other requests
app.get( "*", function( request, response ) {
  response.end( "Opps... Page not found!" );
});

http.createServer( app ).listen( 80 );
```

Writing a desktop HTML5 application

Have you ever wondered about writing a desktop application with HTML5 and JavaScript? Nowadays, we can do this quite easily with NW.js. This project is a cross-platform application runtime based on Chromium and Node.js. So, it provides a frameless browser where both the DOM API and Node.js API are available. In other words, we can run NW.js classical web-applications, access low-level APIs (filesystem, network, processes, and so on), and reuse the modules of the NPM repository. Interesting? We'll start a tutorial where we will create a simple HTML5 application and run it with NW.js. It'll be a roster application with a form to enter names and a list of already submitted ones. The names will be stored in localStorage. Let's rock it.

Setting up the project

First of all, we have to download the NW.js run-time relevant to our platform (Mac OS X, Windows, or Linux) from `http://nwjs.io`. Next to the NW.js executable (`nw.exe`, `new.app`, or `nw.` depending on the platform), we place the `package,json` file (`https://github.com/nwjs/nw.js/wiki/manifest-format`) where we describe our project:

```
{
    "name": "roster",
    "main": "wwwroot/index.html",
    "window": {
        "title": "The Roster",
        "icon": "wwwroot/roaster.png",
        "position": "center",
        "resizable": false,
        "toolbar": false,
        "frame": false,
        "focus": true,
        "width": 800,
        "height": 600,
        "transparent": true
    }
}
```

Our `package.json` file has three main fields. `name` contains a unique name associated with the project. Note that this value will be a part of the directory path where application data (sessionStorage, localStorage, and so on) is stored. `main` accepts a relative path to the main HTML page of the project. Eventually, `window` describes the browser window where the HTML will be displayed.

Adding the HTML5 application

According to the `main` field in `package.json`, we will place our `index.html` in to the `wwwroot` subdirectory. We can try it with a simple HTML like this:

```
<html>
  <body>
    Hello world!
  </body>
</html>
```

NW.js treats the HTML in the same way as a browser, so if we now launch the NW.js executable, we will see `Hello world!`. To give it look and feel we can add CSS and JavaScript. So we can write the code for NW.js in the same way as we do it for a browser. Here, we have a good opportunity to apply the principles that we learned in *Chapter 6, A Large-Scale JavaScript Application Architecture*. In order to make the example concise but expressive, we will take the AngularJS approach. First, we create the HTML. The markup of the body will be as follows:

```
<main class="container">
  <form >
    <div class="form-group">
      <label for="name">Name</label>
      <input class="form-control">
    </div>
    <button class="btn btn-danger">Empty List</button>
    <button type="submit" class="btn btn-primary">Submit</button>
  </form>
  <table class="table table-condensed">
    <tr>
      <td></td>
    </tr>
  </table>
</main>
```

We defined a form to submit new names and a table to display the already stored names. To make it prettier, we used Bootstrap (`http://getbootstrap.com`) styles. The CSS file can be loaded from a CDN as shown here:

```
<link rel="stylesheet" href="https://maxcdn.bootstrapcdn.com/
bootstrap/3.3.5/css/bootstrap.min.css">
```

Now we will bring it to life by adding the AngularJS directives:

```
<html>
<body ng-app="myApp" >
    <main ng-controller="RosterController" class="container">
      <form ng-submit="submit()">
        <div class="form-group">
          <label for="name">Name</label>
          <input class="form-control" id="name" name="name" ng-
model="name" required placeholder="Name">
        </div>
        <button ng-click="empty()" class="btn btn-danger">Empty
List</button>
        <button type="submit" class="btn btn-primary">Submit</
button>
```

```
        </form>
        <table class="table table-condensed">
          <tr ng-repeat="person in persons">
            <td>{{person.value}}</td>
          </tr>
        </table>
      </main>
    </body>
  </html>
```

Here we declares a myApp module scope (<body ng-app="myApp" >). Within this, we defined a RosterController controller. In the boundaries of the controller, we bind our input field to the model name (<input ng-model="name">) and set handlers for the form submit and Empty List button click events (<form ng-submit="submit()"> and <button ng-click="empty()">). Lastly, we make a template bound out of the table to the $scope.persons collection. So whenever the collection changes, the table is updated:

```
<table class="table table-condensed">
  <tr ng-repeat="person in persons">
    <td>{{person.value}}</td>
  </tr>
</table>
```

Now it is time to add some JavaScript to our HTML:

```
<script>
  var app = angular.module( "myApp", [ "ngStorage" ]);

  app.controller("RosterController", function( $scope, $localStorage )
{
    var sync = function() {
      $scope.persons = JSON.parse( $localStorage.persons || "[]" );
    };
    sync();
    $scope.name = "";
    $scope.submit = function() {
      sync();
      $scope.persons.push({ value: $scope.name });
      $localStorage.persons = JSON.stringify( $scope.persons );
    };
    $scope.empty = function() {
      $localStorage.persons = "[]";
      sync();
    };
  });
</script>
```

As we intend to store the data submitted in the form, we can use localStorage that we discussed in *Chapter 4, HTML5 APIs*. In order to get localStorage in the AngularJS way, we used the `ngStorage` module (`https://github.com/gsklee/ngStorage`). So, we specify the plugin during module initialization, and this makes the plugin available in the controller as a parameter (`$localStorage`). In the controller body, we have a function `sync` that sets `$scope.persons` with the person array from localStorage. We call the `sync` function in the form submit handler (`$scope.submit`) and in the **Empty List** button on-click handler (`$scope.empty`). It causes the person table to update every time. During the handling of the submit event, we append the value of the `$scope.persons` input and save `$scope.persons` in localStorage.

In order to enable this functionality, we have to load the AngularJS and ngStorage plugins:

```
<script src="http://ajax.googleapis.com/ajax/libs/angularjs/1.3.14/
angular.min.js"></script>

<script src="https://cdnjs.cloudflare.com/ajax/libs/ngStorage/0.3.6/
ngStorage.min.js"></script>
```

Now we launch the NW.js executable and get the application working. Following screenshot shows Roaster example app in NW.js without styles:

It's all nice, but as we run NW.js frameless, we have no way to even close the application. Besides, we cannot drag the application window within the desktop. This is easy to fix. We can add an HTML fragment to the HTML body with two buttons to close and minimize the application:

```
<header ng-controller="ToolbarController">
  <a href="#" ng-click="minimize()">Minimize</a>
  <a href="#" ng-click="close()">Close</a>
</header>
```

Now we subscribe listeners to these buttons that call the close and minimize NW.js Window API (`https://github.com/nwjs/nw.js/wiki/Window`) methods respectively:

```
var win = require( "nw.gui" ).Window.get();
app.controller("ToolbarController", function( $scope ) {
  $scope.close = function(){
    win.close();
  };
  $scope.minimize = function(){
    win.minimize();
  };
});
```

In order to make our window drag-able (`https://github.com/nwjs/nw.js/wiki/Frameless-window`), we can use the `-webkit-app-region` CSS pseudo-class. We set this with the drag value on the handle container (header) and with the no-drag value on any clickable elements within it:

```
header {
   -webkit-app-region: drag;
}
header a {
   -webkit-app-region: no-drag;
}
```

In addition, we prettify the look and feel of the page. Note that with NW.js, we can have a transparent background. So we set the `border-radius` on the `html` element and the window gets rounded:

```
html {
 height: 100%;
 border-radius: 20px;
 background-color: rgba(0,0,0,0);
}
body {
  min-height: 100%;
  background: linear-gradient(to bottom,  #deefff 0%,#98bede 100%);
  overflow: auto;
}
header {
  text-align: right;
  width: auto;
  padding: 12px;
  background: rgba(255,255,255, 0.5);
  border-radius: 20px 20px 0 0;
```

```
    -webkit-app-region: drag;
  }
header a {
  margin: 12px;
    -webkit-app-region: no-drag;
}
```

Now we can launch our NW.js executable again. Roaster example app in NW.js with styles is shown in the following screenshot:

Note that on Mac OS X/Linux, we have to launch with special arguments (`https://github.com/nwjs/nw.js/wiki/Transparency`) to get the transparency effect. For example, we have to do the following on Mac OS X:

```
open -n ./nwjs.app --args --enable-transparent-visuals –disable-gpu
```

Debugging

Still something is missing. If anything goes wrong, how can we debug and trace the errors? There are a few options available:

- Launch the NW.js executable with the `--enable-logging` argument and get the logs in `stdout`.

- Launch the NW.js executable with `--remote-debugging-port` and access the DevTools application in a remotely running Chrome. For instance, we start up the project as `nw --remote-debugging-port=9222` and look for the `http://localhost:9222` page in Chrome.

- Enable toolbar and frame for the window in `package.json`.

The first option isn't quite handy in debugging. The second provides you with a limited version of DevTools, and the last option brings the frame and can make the application look terrible. Fortunately, we can call DevTools programmatically from the app. So, on the DEVELOPMENT/TEST environment, you can add this code that shows up DevTools by pressing *Ctrl + Shift + I*:

```
console.info( "Here we go!" );

document.addEventListener( "keydown", function( e ){
  var key = parseInt( e.key || e.keyCode, 10 );
  // Ctrl-Shift-i
  if ( e.ctrlKey && e.shiftKey && key === 73 ) {
    e.preventDefault();
    win.showDevTools();
  }
}, false );
```

Programmatically called DevTools in NW.JS are shown in the following screenshot:

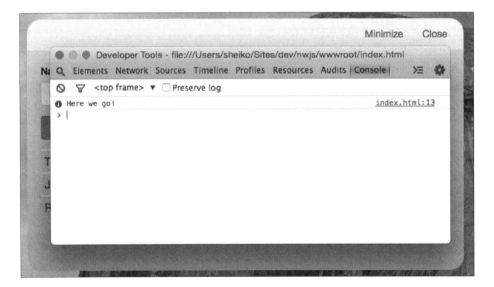

Packaging

To have a real desktop application experience, we can bundle the projects assets and NW.js files into a single executable. Firstly using ZIP, we compress our project directory (`wwwroot`) and the accompanying files (the `node_modules` directory and the `NAPI` plugins) into `app.nw`. Then, we combine the archive with the NW.js executable. In Windows, this can be done as follows:

```
run copy /b nw.exe+app.nw app.exe
```

If the distribution of NW.js that is targeted for your platform contains any components (for example, the Windows distribution includes DLLs), inject them into the newly created application executable using Enigma Virtual Box (`http://enigmaprotector.com`). Voilà, now we can distribute the project in a single file.

Using PhoneGap to make a mobile native app

Well, now we can make desktop applications with JavaScript but what about native mobile applications? There are a number of web-based frameworks available for mobile development (`https://en.wikipedia.org/wiki/Multiple_phone_web-based_application_framework`). One of the most trending solutions is called Adobe PhoneGap, which is built on top of the Apache Cordova project. By and large, the PhoneGap application consists of a web-stack (HTML5, CSS, and JavaScript). Despite the fact that nowadays, HTML5 provides access to some of the native features (accelerometer, camera, contacts, vibration, GPS, and others), the support across different devices is inconsistent and quirky, and performance is relatively poor. So PhoneGap runs HTML5 inside a native WebView on a device and provides access to device resources and APIs (`https://en.wikipedia.org/wiki/Foreign_function_interface`). As a result, we can write a mobile application based on HTML5 and build it with PhoneGap for the devices and OS that we support (iPhone, Android, Blackberry, Windows, Ubuntu, Firefox OS, and others). A good point here is that we can reuse the components created for the Web while developing for mobile. In fact, we can bundle the Roster application that we made for NW.js as a mobile app. So let's do this.

Setting up the project

First of all we need a framework. The easiest way to install it is by using the NPM tool:

```
npm install -g cordova
```

The `-g` option means that we install this globally on the machine and don't need to do it when setting up any new project.

Now we can create a new project with the following command:

```
cordova create roster org.tempuri.roster Roster
```

In the `roster` subdirectory, the tool creates a `boilerplate` file structure for the project named `Roster` that is registered within the `org.tempuri.roster` namespace.

Now, we need to inform PhoneGap about the platforms that we want to support. So, we navigate to the `roster` subdirectory and type the following:

```
cordova platform add ios
cordova platform add android
```

Building the project

In the www subdirectory, we can find a placeholder HTML5 application. We can replace this with the roster application written for NW.js (without an environment-specific header container and its listeners code, of course). In order to check whether the project was properly initialized, we run the following:

```
cordova build ios
cordova emulate ios
```

Alternatively, we can use this:

```
cordova build android
cordova emulate android
```

This builds the project and displays it with a platform-specific emulator. On a Mac, this is how it looks. Roster example app by PhoneGap is shown in the following screenshot:

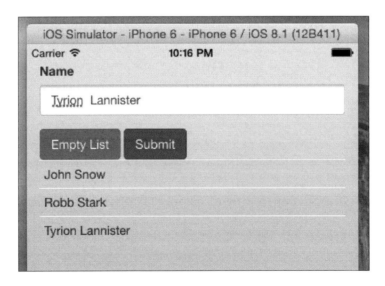

Adding plugins

As it was mentioned already, with PhoneGap, we can access native device features (http://phonegap.com/about/feature). Moreover, we can also install and use native plugins available in the Cordova repository (http://plugins.cordova.io/npm/index.html). Let's take one of these — *cordova-plugin-vibration*. We can add it to the project as easy as this:

```
cordova plugin add cordova-plugin-vibration
```

As we have the plugin, we can use its API in our JavaScript code:

```
// Vibrate for 3 seconds
navigator.vibrate(3000);
```

Debugging

As for debugging a mobile application, there are a number of options (https://github.com/phonegap/phonegap/wiki/Debugging-in-PhoneGap). The main idea is to reach the application with a desktop inspector tool. In the case of iOS, we go with the Safari WebInspector desktop. Just find the **iPhone Simulator** option in the **Develop** menu and press **WebView** corresponding to your application HTML. Similarly, we can access Android WebView in Chrome DevTools (https://developer.chrome.com/devtools/docs/remote-debugging#debugging-webviews).

Summary

The widely spread Node.js run-time extends JavaScript with a low-level API, which unlocks for us on the methods of creating command-line tools, web-servers, and specialized servers (for example UDP-TCP/WebSocket/SSE servers). To see how far we can go beyond the Web, just consider a standalone OS NodeOS built with Node.js. With HTML5 and JavaScript we can write a desktop software and easily distribute it across different platforms. Similarly, we can compose a mobile application out of HTML5/JavaScript and native APIs. Using tools such as PhoneGap, we can build the application for diverse mobile platforms.

In this chapter, we learned how to access DevTools to debug NW.js and PhoneGap applications. In the next chapter, we will talk about how to use DevTools efficiently.

8
Debugging and Profiling

Debugging is a tricky part of programming. Bugs during development are unavoidable. Whatever our experience, we have to spend quite a time on hunting them. It happens. By the looks of the code you may not find the bug, there probably must be no problem with the application, yet a developer fights for hours until they run into a silly reason such as a misprinted property name. Much of this time could be saved by making a better use of browser development tools. So we will consider in this chapter the following topics:

- How to discover bugs
- Getting the best from a console API
- How to tune performance

Hunting bugs

Debugging is about finding and resolving defects that prevent the intended application behavior. Here, what is crucial is to find the code causing the problem. What do we usually do when we encounter a bug? Let's say, we have a form that is assumed to run a validation on a submit event, but it doesn't. First of all, we have a number of assumptions to be met. For example, if the reference to the form element is valid, if the event and method name were spelled correctly during registering a listener, if the object context is not lost in the body of the listener, and so on.

Some bugs can be discovered automatically such as by validating input and output on the entry and exit points of methods (see Design by contract at: https://en.wikipedia.org/wiki/Design_by_contract). However, we have to spot other bugs manually, and here we can use two options. Starting from the point where the code is surely correct step by step to the problem point (bottom-up debugging), or on the contrary, stepping back from the break point to find the source of the break. Here, browser development tools can come in handy.

The most advanced one is Chrome DevTools. We can open the **Sources** panel in it and set breakpoints in the code. The browser stops execution while reaching a breakpoint and shows a pane with an actual variable scope and call stack. It also provides controls that one can use to *step-through* the code back and forth one line at a time. Following screenshot shows debugging with the help of breakpoints:

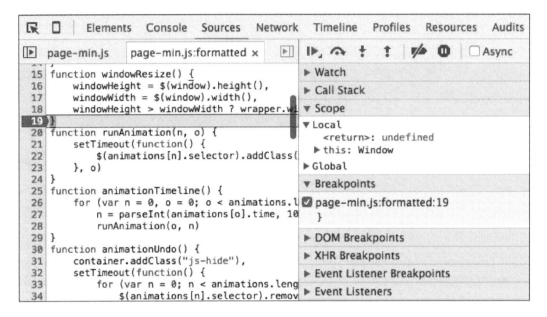

However, this can be tricky to navigate through codebase in DevTools. Fortunately, you can set a break point out of the browser directly in the IDE. You just need to put the debugger statement on the line where you want the browser to break.

Sometimes, it is hard to figure out what's going on with the DOM. We can make DevTools to do a break on the DOM events such as node removal, node modification, and subtree changes. Just navigate to the HTML element in the **Sources** panel, right-click, and choose the **Break on...** option.

Besides, in the **Source** panel there is a tab called **XHR Breakpoints** where we can set a list of URLs. The browser will then break when any of the URLs are requested.

You can also find an icon in form of stop sign in the top of **Source** panel sidebar. If this button is clicked, DevTools will break on any caught exception and bring to you the throw location in the source code. Following screenshot shows how to use Pause on Caught Exception tool:

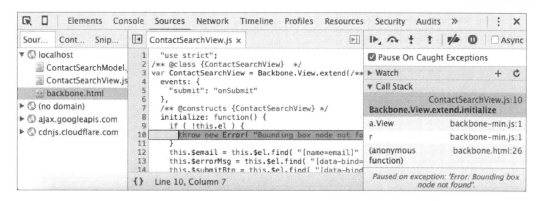

 For more information, see `https://developer.chrome.com/devtools/docs/javascript-debugging`.

Getting the best from a console API

Despite it being not a part of JavaScript, we all use console API extensively to find out what is really happening during an app life cycle. The API, once introduced by the Firebug tool, is now available in every major JavaScript agent. Most developers just do simple logging using methods such as error, trace, log, and the decorator such as info and warn. Well, when we pass any values to `console.log`, they are presented to the **JavaScript Console** panel. Usually, we pass a string describing a case and a list of various objects that we want to inspect. However, did you know that we can refer to these objects directly from the string in the manner of the PHP `sprintf`? So the string given as the first argument can be a template that contains format specifiers for the rest of the arguments:

```javascript
var node = document.body;
console.log( "Element %s has %d child nodes; JavaScript object %O, DOM
element %o",
  node.tagName,
  node.childNodes.length,
  node,
  node );
```

The available specifiers are `%s` for strings, `%d` for numbers, `%o` for DOM elements, and `%O` for JavaScript objects (the same as `console.dir`). Besides, there is a particular specifier that allows us to style the `console.log` report. This can be very useful. In practice, the application console receives too many log records. It gets hard to make out the desired messages among a hundred similar messages. What we can do is categorize the messages and style them accordingly:

```
console.log.user = function(){
  var args = [].slice.call( arguments );
  args.splice( 0, 0, "%c USER ",
    "background-color: #7DB4B5; border-radius: 3px; color: #fff;
font-weight: bold; " );
  console.log.apply( console, args );
};

console.log.event = function(){
  var args = [].slice.call( arguments );
  args.splice( 0, 0, "%c EVENT ",
    "background-color: #f72; border-radius: 3px; color: #fff; font-
weight: bold; " );
  console.log.apply( console, args );
};
console.log( "Generic log record" );
console.log.user( "User click button Foo" );
console.log.event( "Bar triggers `Baz` event on Qux" );
```

In this example, we defined two methods extending `console.log`. One prefixes console messages with **USER** on cyan and is intended for user action events. The second prepends reports with **EVENT** and is meant to highlight mediator events. Following screenshot explains colorized output with console.log:

Another lesser known trick is the use of `console.assert` for assertions in code logic. So, we assume that a condition is true and until it is everything is fine and we get no messages. But as soon as it fails, we get a record in the console:

```
console.assert( sessionId > 0, "Session is created" );
```

Following screenshot shows how to use console assertions:

Sometimes we need to know how often an event happens. Here we can use the `console.count` method:

```
function factory( constr ){
    console.count( "Factory is called for " + constr );
    // return new window[ constr ]();
}
factory( "Foo" );
factory( "Bar" );
factory( "Foo" );
```

This displays in the console the specified message and an auto-updating counter next to it. Following screenshot shows how to use console.count:

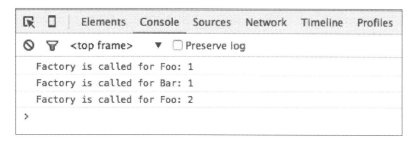

 You can find out more about working with the console at `https://developer.chrome.com/devtools/docs/console`.

Tuning performance

Performance makes user experience. If it takes too long to load a page or a UI to respond, the user is likely to leave the application and never come back. It's especially true with web apps. In *Chapter 3, DOM Scripting and AJAX*, we compared different approaches to manipulate the DOM. In order to find out how fast an approach is, we use a performance built-in object:

```
"use strict";
var cpuExpensiveOperation = function(){
    var i = 100000;
    while( --i ) {
      document.body.appendChild( document.createElement( "div" ) );
    }
  },
  // Start test time
  s = performance.now();

cpuExpensiveOperation();
console.log( "Process took", performance.now() - s, "ms" );
```

`performance.now()` returns a high resolution timestamp that represents time in milliseconds accurate to microseconds. This is designed and widely used for benchmarking. However, a `time/timeEnd` console object also provides methods to measure time:

```
console.time( "cpuExpensiveOperation took" );
cpuExpensiveOperation();
console.timeEnd( "cpuExpensiveOperation took" );
```

Following screenshot shows measuring time with console:

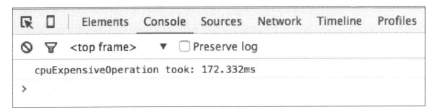

If we need to know what exactly is going on during an operation execution, we can request a profile for that period:

```
console.profile( "cpuExpensiveOperation" );
cpuExpensiveOperation();
console.profileEnd( "cpuExpensiveOperation" );
```

Following screenshot shows how to use console API for profiling:

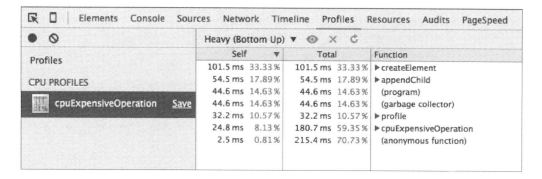

Moreover, we can mark the exact time of the event in the **Timeline** panel of DevTools:

```
cpuExpensiveOperation();
console.timeStamp( "cpuExpensiveOperation finished" );
```

Following screenshot shows how to mark events on Timeline during a recording session:

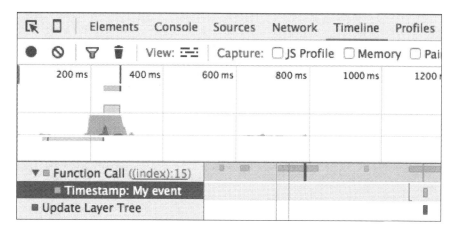

When tuning performance, we have to pay particular attention to the response time. There are a number of techniques that can be used to improve user experience during bootstrap (non-blocking JavaScript and CSS loading, critical CSS, moving static files CDN, and others). Well, let's say you decide to load CSS asynchronously (`https://www.npmjs.com/package/asynccss`) and cache into localStorage. But how would you test whether you gained anything from this? Fortunately, DevTools has a filmstrip feature. We just need to open the **Network** panel, enable **Screenshot capturing** and reload the page.

DevTools shows us the progress of the page load frame after frame as the user sees the page during the load process. Besides, we can manually set a connection speed (throttling) for a test and find out how it affects the filmstrip. Following screenshot shows how to getting filmstrip of page loading:

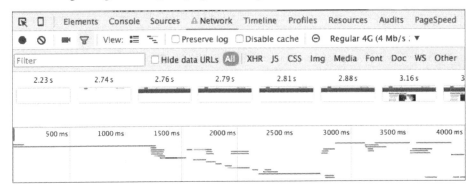

Summary

Debugging is an integral part of web development. It can also be a pretty sluggish and tedious task. With browser development tools, we can reduce the time spent on hunting bugs. We can set breakpoints in a code and move step by step to the source of the problem in the same way that the program does. When using Chrome DevTools, we can watch for DOM modification events and for specific URL requests. When tuning performance, we can measure time with `time/timeEnd` and request a process profile with `profile/profileEnd`. Using features such as filmstrip and throttling, we can look at the page load on different connections.

We started this book by reviewing JavaScript core features. We've learned how to make a code more expressive by means of syntactic sugar, practiced object iteration and collection normalization, compared various approaches to declare an object including ES6 classes, and found out how to use the *magic methods* of JavaScript. Then, we dived into modular programming. We talked about module pattern and modules in general and reviewed three main approaches to modularization in JavaScript AMD, CommonJS, and ES6 modules. The next topic was about keeping high-performance DOM manipulations. We also examined Fetch API. We also considered some of most exciting HTML5 APIs such Storage, IndexedDB, workers, SSE, and WebSocket, and the technologies under the hood of Web Component. We considered techniques to leverage a JavaScript event loop and to build nonblocking applications. We practiced with design patterns in JavaScript and covered concern separations. We wrote a simple application in three frameworks, Backbone, Angular, and React. We tried out Node.js by creating a command-line utility and exposing a web server. We also created a demo desktop application with NW.js and its mobile version with PhoneGap. At last, we talked about bug hunting.

Index

Thank you for buying
Javascript Unlocked

About Packt Publishing

Packt, pronounced 'packed', published its first book, *Mastering phpMyAdmin for Effective MySQL Management*, in April 2004, and subsequently continued to specialize in publishing highly focused books on specific technologies and solutions.

Our books and publications share the experiences of your fellow IT professionals in adapting and customizing today's systems, applications, and frameworks. Our solution-based books give you the knowledge and power to customize the software and technologies you're using to get the job done. Packt books are more specific and less general than the IT books you have seen in the past. Our unique business model allows us to bring you more focused information, giving you more of what you need to know, and less of what you don't.

Packt is a modern yet unique publishing company that focuses on producing quality, cutting-edge books for communities of developers, administrators, and newbies alike. For more information, please visit our website at www.packtpub.com.

About Packt Open Source

In 2010, Packt launched two new brands, Packt Open Source and Packt Enterprise, in order to continue its focus on specialization. This book is part of the Packt Open Source brand, home to books published on software built around open source licenses, and offering information to anybody from advanced developers to budding web designers. The Open Source brand also runs Packt's Open Source Royalty Scheme, by which Packt gives a royalty to each open source project about whose software a book is sold.

Writing for Packt

We welcome all inquiries from people who are interested in authoring. Book proposals should be sent to author@packtpub.com. If your book idea is still at an early stage and you would like to discuss it first before writing a formal book proposal, then please contact us; one of our commissioning editors will get in touch with you.

We're not just looking for published authors; if you have strong technical skills but no writing experience, our experienced editors can help you develop a writing career, or simply get some additional reward for your expertise.

Mastering JavaScript Design Patterns

ISBN: 978-1-78398-798-6   Paperback: 290 pages

Discover how to use JavaScript design patterns to create powerful applications with reliable and maintainable code

1. Learn how to use tried and true software design methodologies to enhance your Javascript code.

2. Discover robust JavaScript implementations of classic as well as advanced design patterns.

3. Packed with easy-to-follow examples that can be used to create reusable code and extensible designs.

Reactive Programming with JavaScript

ISBN: 978-1-78355-855-1   Paperback: 264 pages

Learn the hot new frontend web framework from Facebook – ReactJS, an easy way of developing the V in MVC and a better approach to software engineering in JavaScript

1. Learn to develop webapps for Facebook's front-end development using ReactJS.

2. Use functional reactive programming with ReactJS.

3. Easy to understand, comprehensive with in-depth coverage of practical examples.

Please check **www.PacktPub.com** for information on our titles

Functional Programming
in JavaScript

ISBN: 978-1-78439-822-4   Paperback: 172 pages

Unlock the powers of functional programming hidden within JavaScript to build smarter, cleaner, and more reliable web apps

1. Discover what functional programming is, why it's effective, and how it's used in JavaScript.

2. Understand and optimize JavaScript's hidden potential as a true functional language.

3. Explore the best coding practices for real-world applications.

JavaScript at Scale

ISBN: 978-1-78528-215-7   Paperback: 266 pages

Build enduring JavaScript applications with scaling insights from the front-line of JavaScript development

1. Design and implement JavaScript application architectures that scale from a number of perspectives, such as addressability, configurability, and performance.

2. Understand common JavaScript scaling pitfalls and how to tackle them through practical, real-world, solutions and strategies.

3. Learn techniques to deliver reusable architectures that stand the test of time.

Please check **www.PacktPub.com** for information on our titles

Made in the USA
Middletown, DE
16 October 2017